RENAISSANCE COMIC TALES
of Love, Treachery, and Revenge

છ૭

RENAISSANCE COMIC TALES
of Love, Treachery, and Revenge

☙

Edited and Translated from Italian
with an Introduction by
Valerie Martone &
Robert L. Martone

ITALICA PRESS
NEW YORK
1994

ITALICA PRESS, INC.

595 Main Street
New York, New York 10044

Library of Congress Cataloging-in-Publication Data
Renaissance comic tales of love, treachery, and revenge / [Gentile
    Sermini ... et al.] ; edited and translated from Italian with an
    introduction by Valerie Martone & Robert L. Martone.
        p.   cm.
    Includes bibliographical references.
    ISBN 0-934977-31-3
        1. Short stories, Italian – Translations into English. 2. Italian
    fiction – To 1400 – Translations into English.s. 3. Italian fiction – 15th
    century – Translations into English. 4. Italian fiction – 16th century
    – Translations into English. 5. Novelle. I. Sermini, Gentile, 15th cent.
    II. Martone, Valerie, 1957-   . III. Martone, Robert L., 1960-   .
    PQ4257.E5R46 1994
    853'.0108 – dc20   94-16287
                                                                    CIP

Printed in the United States of America
5 4 3 2 1

ABOUT THE TRANSLATORS

Valerie Martone received her Masters degree from
Columbia University. She works as an editor. Robert
L. Martone is a research scientist. Both received their
undergraduate degrees from the State University of
New York at Albany and have lived and studied in
Italy. They previously translated Antonio Manetti's
The Fat Woodworker, also published by Italica Press.

Prologo

OME CHE io manifesta mente com prenda e per indubitato te ga iclita e ex celsa madon na che al so- no de la mia bassa e raucha lita nö si cöue gha de libro comporre ne meno de proprio no- me intitularlo : e che piu de temerita dignamente sero redarguito che dal cuna eloquentia ne molto ne pocho commendato : Nondimeno hauen- do da la mia tenera eta saticato per exercitio del mio grosso e rudissimo ingegno e della pigra e roza mano scripte alcune nouelle per autentiche hiftorie approbate negli moderni & antiqui tempi trauenute : e quelle ad diuerse digniffime persone per me mandare si come chiaro nelli loro ti toli se dimostra . Per la cui chagione ho uoluto quelle cheran gia disperse congregare e de esse insieme unite fa bricare il presente libretto & quello per la sua pocha qualita nominare il Nouellino . Et ad solo presidio e lume della nostra italica regione in

CONTENTS

Contents

ILLUSTRATIONS

INTRODUCTION

꽃

The Italian Renaissance was a period characterized by a revival of interest in ancient texts that precipitated a self-conscious effort toward spiritual, cultural, and political rebirth, and the stories of the Italian *novelliere* provide an insight into the spirit of this time. Whether the author was a Florentine or a native of the distant state of Naples the compositions reveal a fundamental kinship of impulse and spirit. These are writers who scorned personal risk to expose the follies of princes and clerics with a veracious pen. These are the writings of Renaissance authors who were so keenly aware of history and their place in it and so conscious of their debt to the future that they collected and preserved volumes of stories. These are the writings of Italians who were inspired by sheer love of their language to exalt it through their works.

The birth of prose fiction in the form of the *novella* is closely associated with the *Decameron* of Giovanni Boccaccio (1313-65). This popular collection of tales found wide appeal among the burgeoning and highly successful merchant class of the Renaissance. Indeed, the *Decameron* came to be known as a "mercantile epic" because it was written in prose for this new, non-courtly audience. One of its intended purposes was to provide pleasant entertainment in the spoken language of the people. According to the mid-century viewpoint of

Charles Singleton, the art of Boccaccio's tales was the art of escape because "they could not claim to teach,"[1] as did moral *exempla* or logical arguments. Boccaccio's use of comic paradox and irony and his escape from exemplary tradition freed his stories "from any absolute interpretive systems and cleared a new non-dogmatic fictional space."[2] Thus, the *novella* became a window through which to view popular culture. Since Boccaccio's time, this "new thing," the novella, has offered a progressive and dynamic avenue of expression in a changing society.

Along with that of Dante (1265-1321) and Petrarch (1304-74), Boccaccio's use of the vernacular as a literary medium elevated the spoken language and allowed the author to express a pride in his native tongue. The *Decameron* set the standard for this new literary language and literature, and many of the *novellieri* who followed in Boccaccio's footsteps praised him as their master. Giovanni Gherardi da Prato,[3] for example, placed Boccaccio beside Dante and Petrarch as one of the "three Florentine crowns" of literature, while Antonfrancesco Grazzini[4] called him "San Giovanni Boccadoro" (Saint John Golden-Mouth). Some chose a more sincere form of flattery: imitation of Boccaccio's stories with only trivial embellishment or superficial changes. Many modeled their own collections after Boccaccio's example by organizing their stories within a thematic arrangement, such as Firenzuola's *Tales*, Masuccio Salernitano's[5] *Novellino*, and Gherardi da Prato's *Paradiso degli Alberti*. Chaucer, too, imitated Boccaccio's lively style in his *Canterbury Tales*, proof of the international appeal of the novella.[6] Like Boccaccio's tales, the stories included in the present collection resonate with Italian folklore, earthy humor, and the flavor of everyday life.

The characters in these stories portray both historical figures and burlesque characters possessed by archetypal human motivation who often achieve their ends by deception. Love motivates Montanina to feign death in "Montanina's Deception." Revenge is the motive behind a meal of filthy drawers for Bindaccino in the story of "Bindaccino da Fiesole," and the cause of Neri Chiaramontesi's madness in "A Trick Played by the Scheggia on Neri Chiaramontesi." Nothing can match the sheer intellectual delight of "the pleasing fellow" when, with his capricious wit, he encounters a blithering simpleton and weaves around him a treacherous plot. Treachery itself can be a motive, and the humorous results are as entertaining today as when these tales were originally told for the enjoyment of pleasant companions around a banquet table.

Humor was the subject of a discourse by Baldassare Castiglione (1478–1529) in *The Book of the Courtier* (1528). Castiglione asserted that humor was such a fundamental characteristic of human nature that a human being could be defined simply as "an animal capable of laughing." He wrote, "everything which provokes laughter exalts a man's spirit and gives him pleasure," so that the person who inspires laughter "deserves every praise."[7] Following the example of Cicero, who discussed humor in *On the Orator*, Castiglione does not refuse the nearly irresistible impulse to embellish his discourse on humor with his favorite jokes and stories, which nearly fill the second book of his masterpiece. Like Cicero, Castiglione classifies the "pleasantries" that elicit laughter by distinguishing between the quick remark, such as a pun or cutting reply, and those that are developed into a long narrative. But Castiglione deviates from his Latin model by creating a third category among the spectrum of humorous archetypes, the *beffa*, or practical joke.[8] It is remarkable that Castiglione chose to single out practical jokes as one of the principle varieties of pleasantries, but the prodigious wealth of practical jokes found among the stories of the *novellieri* might lead one to believe that life in Renaissance Italy was lived at great peril. Indeed, Jacob Burckhardt was led to this assumption and declared in his *Civilization of the Renaissance in Italy* that, "Italy had, in fact become a school for scandal [in which] the general culture of the time had educated a poisonous brood of impotent wits, of born critics and railers...an easy-going contempt of everything and everybody was probably the prevailing tone of society."[9]

The trickster is an enduring character, however, and there can be no doubt that the *novellieri* held their "pleasant fellows" in the highest regard. Antonio Manetti (1423-97), for example, composed his story, *Il Grasso Legnaiuolo* (*The Fat Woodworker*),[10] as a testament to the genius of Filippo Brunelleschi. Manetti was an ardent admirer of the Florentine architect who built the cupola of the cathedral of Florence and who, in the words of the architect Antonio Averlino, called "Filarete," "found by reason what the mirror showed"[11] with his invention of the method of artificial perspective. Whether *The Fat Woodworker* was based upon facts, as some contend, or entirely contrived, it is clear that Manetti found Brunelleschi's cunning talent of deception a most admirable quality. Likewise, Grazzini extolled the pranks

Introduction

played by the artist Masaccio's brother, the Scheggia; and both Franco Sacchetti (1333-1400) and Matteo Bandello[12] celebrated the singular exploits of the trickster Gonnella.

Although Renaissance Italy may have seen the craft of the sly trickster developed into high art, Mediterranean culture itself was imbued with subtle strains of the trickster's character. The word *beffa*, for example, is also reminiscent of *Befana*, the name of the ugly witch who delivers toys to good children on the epinomous feast, Epiphany.[13] The Befana was endowed with Saturnalian powers of transformation and could change any child who awoke during her visit into any person or thing that the child desired, simply for the asking.

The magic of the winter season was well known to the authors of these stories and they paid particular attention to it. The Florentine expatriates in Gherardi's story of "Berto and More," for example, were so amazed by what they saw during their visit to Hungary that they exclaimed that it was "as if it were the feast of the Epiphany." The first of Grazzini's three *Cene* or "Dinner Parties" takes place during a winter snowstorm, when it is decided to continue dining and storytelling on the two successive Thursdays of Carnival. Other stories like Grazzini's "A Trick Played by the Scheggia Upon Neri Chiaramontesi" take place during "the heart of winter" and thereby partake of the illusory nature of this season as well. Of course, it is also impossible to overlook the connection between storytelling in general and this time of year when the days are shortest and life contracts around the hearth fires and dining tables.

The Italian *novelle* of the Renaissance enjoyed an international audience, and the stories were frequently adapted by contemporary French and English writers. Geoffrey Bullough [14] cites numerous *novelle* as antecedents to Shakespearean theater. Shakespeare's *Two Gentlemen of Verona,* for example, was an adaptation of a *novella* from the *Decameron* (Day 10, Story 8), while a *novella* from Sir Giovanni Fiorentino's *Il Pecorone* inspired Shakespeare's *Merchant of Venice.* Italian *novelle* were so popular among the English, and so frequently adapted for the stage that the sixteenth-century author Stephen Gosson complained that such stories were being "ransacked to furnish the play houses in London." The collection of *novelle* presented here contains antecedents of, or stories related to, Shakespeare's *Romeo and Juliet* and *Twelfth Night.*

The Italian Renaissance not only provided a literary resource for the English stage, but also a philosophical foundation. As Frances Yates asserted in her *Theatre of the World,* "the London theater movement [was] in some way connected to the revival of the ancient [Roman] theater, stemming from the recovery of Vitruvius in Italy.... The inference seems obvious that this was...a Renaissance return to antiquity...to the old theater of Rome." [15] In Yates's analysis, the English theaters of Shakespeare's time, such as the Globe Theatre, were an expression of the place of men and women in the world (hence the phrase "all the world's a stage"), and were part of the Renaissance philosophical and architectural movements that took place throughout Europe with origins in Italy.

The influence of Renaissance Italian tales on European literature was profound because here we discover many of the important roots of narrative fiction, which was to become one of the most significant forms of post-medieval literature. The following selection of sixteen tales represents only a small portion of the hundreds written, but they were selected to present a diverse picture of this cultural legacy. Their six authors are from various regions of the Italian peninsula; and while each of them shares a peculiar sense of humor, their individual lives, styles, and perspectives contribute to the richness of this genre.

The Authors

In the historical record, Gentile Sermini is little more than a name attached to a collection of writings composed early in the fifteenth century. The date of Sermini's work is provided by his statement in *Novella* 12 that, "in the year 1424 I was fleeing the plague, not unlike a poisoned fish that makes for the sea, when I arrived in a hillock of our countryside. I lodged there because the place was free of disease." It may be surmised that this Sienese author was wealthy and well-educated from his statement about his relationship with Giovanni Gherardi da Prato: "we had been business acquaintances and friends for a long time, since we attended the university together." His manuscript was written anonymously and dedicated to his dear and anonymous brother in Bagno a Petriolo, and his collection of writings was deliberately assembled without any care for order: just as when making a salad, he wrote, "you put the greens in the bowl when you find them, mixing them up without distinction." Mixed among the forty *novelle* are a dedicatory letter to his

Introduction

brother, a letter to Venus, a description of a game of fighting, as well as several *canzoni* and sonnets. His intention in undertaking these compositions, clearly stated in his first *novella*, was to preserve those stories he heard and most esteemed so they would be as fresh in future years as when the events first happened or when the stories were first told. That first *novella* met Sermini's intentions beyond measure, because "Montanina's Deception," presented here, is, perhaps, the first written version of the story of Romeo and Juliet.

The pedigree of such an archetypal story is quite complex, and there are a number of antecedents or stories related to Shakespeare's *Romeo and Juliet* in the Italian *novelle* of this period. Bandello's *Novelle* 2.40 and 2.41, Masuccio's *Novellino* 33, and Grazzini's *Cene* 2.2 all partake of the same central motif of Sermini's story. These stories are stages in the metamorphosis from oral tradition to written literature, and from comedy to tragedy. While Sermini uses the device of the live burial as an excuse to indulge in some ribald anticlericalism, Grazzini takes the same device to ludicrous extreme in "Mariotto's Burning Desire to Die" with the idiotic Mariotto crying, "Carry me away and bury me. Carry me away because I am dead." The originally comic stories of Sermini and Bandello evolve into tragedy in the hands of Masuccio. The story is given a historical context by Luigi da Porto in his *Storia di Due Nobili Amanti,* which was translated into French, and then into English before being received by Shakespeare.

In composing his stories, Sermini did not display any particular concern with historical relevance, or with the development of characters, but he showed great interest

Introduction

in expressing action. A clear illustration of this is his
"Description of a Boxing Match":

> "Run over here. Don't stop. Turn here. There they
> are, let me up front. Come on. Come on. Hit him
> there. Who's fighting?" "I am." "And I." "Hit him.
> Ah, ah, that was good! Now like so. To the jaw. To
> the hip. Hit him low. Ah, ah, ah, good match, good
> match!"

The story of "Bindaccino da Fiesole" possesses a similar
vivacity and resembles stories by Sacchetti (*Trecentonovelle*
98), Piovano Arlotto (*Motti e Facezie* 156) and Bandello
(*Novelle* 2.1). The second of Sermini's *novelle* selected
here, however, provides an important exception: it is
unique in that it presents a historical figure, Giovanni
Gherardi da Prato (called Acquettino, 1367–1446?).
Gherardi was the author of *Il Paradiso degli Alberti*, the
source of two stories presented in this collection,
"Dolcibene" and "Berto and More."

Gherardi was a popular target of satire, not only by
Sermini but also by Giovanni Fiorentino in *Il Pecorone*, by
the barber poet Domenico di Giovanni, known as
Burchiello, and by the architect Brunelleschi. In *The Fat
Woodworker*, Manetti cast Gherardi as a judge incarcerated
for his debts. In Sermini's story of "Sir Giovanni da Prato
and Baldina," Mona Chiara and her daughter Baldina
were taught how to "write" by a young knight. The
sexual connotations of the narrative are obvious, and
when his "quill" began to fail because it "could not bear
so much writing," Sir Ugolino was approached by
Gherardi, "an expert in the scrivener's art of the notary,"
to arrange a liaison with Baldina. During their encounter,
however, Gherardi, who was notoriously pedantic, be-

came distracted with reading Dante. The miserable failure of his encounter with the lovely Baldina may be an allusion to Gherardi's alleged homosexuality.[16] Gherardi's expertise in vernacular literature received far more appropriate recognition when he was given the prestigious academic appointment as lecturer on Dante at the University of Florence in 1417.

Between the years 1384 and 1388 Gherardi attended the University at Padua and, among such luminaries as Paolo Toscanelli, he was a disciple of the celebrated philosopher Biagio Pelacani. A contestant in the competition for the design of the cathedral dome in Florence, Gherardi later served as a technical advisor to the project, which was awarded to Filippo Brunelleschi. He had the great misfortune, however, of becoming embroiled in a bitter dispute with the architect. Brunelleschi was a notoriously contentious individual: even a dispute with his son required the patient intervention of the pope, and more resilient characters than Gherardi suffered greatly at his hands. The argument between these men was recorded in an exchange of sonnets.[17] In Gherardi's attack upon Brunelleschi, he alludes to a "barge which flies on water," a reference to a barge, invented by Brunelleschi, that was driven by propellers in the water as well as in the air. Laced with Latin phrases, Gherardi's sonnet throws down the gauntlet. He suggests, quite simply, that Brunelleschi is a liar who easily sways the gullible "plebe" with his deceptions. Never one to shrink from an argument, Brunelleschi replies with his own sonnet in which he praises divine inspiration and the gifts of nature over the cowardice of the learned.

In the 1420s, Gherardi suffered the loss first of his lectureship and then of his post as advisor for the construction of the cathedral dome. He retired to compose his most famous work, *Il Paradiso degli Alberti*.

Gherardi left no doubt as to his motive in writing the *Paradiso,* feeling, as he stated, "the ardent desire, which spurs me on incessantly, to exalt our mother-tongue as well as I can and know, and to ennoble it in the way it has already been ennobled and exalted by the three crowns of Florence more than by anybody else."

Composed of five books, *Il Paradiso* was left unfinished and unpublished upon Gherardi's death and, with the passage of time, sections have been lost and the composition has become damaged and mutilated. In the first book, Gherardi narrates a fantastic voyage through the Mediterranean to the island of Cyprus. There, the palace of Venus is described amid stories of the most famous lovers and in discussions upon the nature of love. In the remaining four books, *novelle* are intermixed with the learned philosophical disputations of the most elegant and cultivated members of Florentine society who gathered in 1389, first in the Villa Poppi in Casentino, and later in the villa of Antonio di Niccolo degli Alberti. This mixture of Boccaccian stories with erudite discourse has sometimes been viewed as an intermediate stage between the *Trecento volgare* tradition of Boccaccio, Sachetti, and others, and the works of the classically trained humanists of the Quattrocento. However, Hans Baron disputes Gherardi's claim to any such evolutionary link by citing Gherardi's "lack of originality" and his efforts to superficially imitate the Quattrocento humanists "while [remaining] deeply attached to the intellectual and emotional world of the

Trecento."[18] Nevertheless Baron praised Gherardi, saying that he "made his own contribution by his unswerving love of the Florentine tongue, and by his zeal to prove that there was still room for vernacular culture in a world changed by Quattrocento classicism."

The stories selected here, "Dolcibene" and "Berto and More," are the most energetic and light-hearted of *Il Paradiso,* providing a distraction from its most ponderous philosophical discourses. They owe much to the influence of Franco Sacchetti, to whom Gherardi addressed a sonnet, where he described himself as a "student of law and of poetry."

The story of "Dolcibene" recounts the exploit of Dolcibene de' Tori, a Florentine courtesan and musician who was crowned "King of the Fools" by Emperor Charles IV of Luxembourg. The protagonist in nine of Sacchetti's *Trecentonovelle,* Dolcibene maintained a poetic correspondence with Sacchetti. In this story he had the courage to deceive no less a target than the dreaded tyrant of Milan, Bernabò de' Visconti.

In the story of "Berto and More" two Florentines set out in search of their fortunes in the wealthy country of Hungary. There they prove their idiocy to the delight of the king and the chagrin of their relatives and fellow expatriates. The Florentine *condottiere* Pippo Spano, captain general of Hungary, established a large colony of Florentines in that country where they were well paid for their skills. The Florentine expatriates included luminaries such as Masolino, Masaccio's master. Hungary was occasionally mentioned in Italian *novelle* of the fifteenth century either as a place that promised great wealth, or as a welcome place for exile, as it served for Manetto in *The Fat Woodworker*.

※

If Gherardi da Prato suffered at the hands of Gentile Sermini, it was Sermini and his fellow citizens of Siena who were brazenly attacked by Lorenzo de' Medici in his story of "Giacoppo." The rivalry between Siena and Lorenzo's Florence was made clear when Lorenzo asserted that all Sienese men behave badly so they will seem as ill-bred as their fathers in order to appear to be true, not illegitimate sons.

Lorenzo de' Medici (1449–92) was the quintessential scholar-prince of the Renaissance. Taught from the age of ten by many of the most famous intellectuals of the time, including Marsilio Ficino, Cristoforo Landino, and Poliziano, he assumed powers of state at the age of twenty and ruled until his death in 1492. He was regarded by many historians as a magnanimous and benevolent ruler, much as he is represented by Grazzini in the stories "A Trick Played by the Scheggia on Neri Chiaramontesi," and "Doctor Manente." In the latter story, it was Lorenzo himself who played a joke upon Manente to rid himself of the doctor who often appeared at his dinner table uninvited. This esteem for Lorenzo may be due to a sentimentality for the comparatively peaceful period of Lorenzo's rule, which was followed tragically by the Wars of Italy.

That peaceful time was, however, punctuated by the Pazzi Conspiracy of 1478. Francesco and Girolamo de' Pazzi, members of the powerful Pazzi banking family, had allied themselves with Pope Sixtus IV (Francesco della Rovere) in an attempt to end the Medicean hegemony over Florence. On April 26 of that year Francesco de' Pazzi with the help of Archbishop Salviati, two disgruntled priests – Antonio Maffei and Stefano da Bagnone – and a band of Perugian mercenaries tried to assassinate both Lorenzo and his brother Giuliano during the presentation of the host at mass in the cathedral, Sta. Maria del Fiore. Giuliano died but Lorenzo escaped with minor injuries. When the conspirators were mutilated and hanged, Sixtus retaliated by excommunicating Lorenzo and pronouncing an interdiction against Florence. Sixtus joined forces with the king of Naples to war against Florence, but Lorenzo went, at great personal risk, to see King Ferdinand I of Naples in order to conclude a peace. He succeeded, and the courage he showed in undertaking such an endeavor, as well as the political skill he demon‐strated in bringing it to a successful conclusion, won him enthusiastic support among the Florentines and great prestige abroad. The Pazzi Conspiracy marked a turning point for Lorenzo and was followed by a period of prolific composition. He is best known for his amorous poems, although he was once inspired to parody no less a work than Dante's *Commedia* with his *Simposio* or *I Beoni*. Like the *Commedia*, the *Simposio* begins in a woods described in somber tones:

> In the time of year when every leaf loses its green, and takes on other colors, and when all the trees blanch and then lose each one of their leaves....

But rather than the sublime pilgrimage of Dante, the *Simposio* led to a more mundane destination:

All were going towards the Ponte a Rifredi, because Giannesse had opened a bottle of wine that quickened slow feet.

The story of "Giacoppo" included in this collection is one of Lorenzo's few prose works, and is one of the most famous examples of its genre.

🦁

Matteo Bandello (1485–1561) was one of the preeminent authors of the sixteenth century, and his *Novelle* were among the most important and widely diffused prose works of his time. Bandello was familiar with the most celebrated figures of his day, and he traveled widely in Italy during the first half of the sixteenth century, a tumultuous time when foreign troops vied with one another and with native forces on Italian soil.

Born in Lombardy, in 1497 Bandello entered the Dominican monastery of Santa Maria delle Grazie in Milan where his uncle, Vincenzo, was prior. From this period of his youth he recalled witnessing Leonardo paint his famous *Last Supper*. In 1504 he took vows and the following year accompanied his uncle, then general of the Dominican Order, on an inspection tour of Dominican monasteries in central and southern Italy. His travels took him as far south as Calabria where in 1506 his uncle died. After returning to Milan, he entered the services of Alessandro Bentivoglio, son of Giovanni Bentivoglio, then lord of Milan when that city was the capital of French occupation in Italy. He became a diplomatic agent for Alessandro, traveling to Blois and Lyon on his behalf in 1508, but when French influence in the region failed four years later he became a supporter of Massimiliano Sforza. His fortune changed quickly, however, and when the French returned to power in 1515 after the battle of Melegnano, Bandello was forced to flee Milan for the safety of Mantova where he found protection in the court of Isabella d'Este. Later, when the French were forced from the region after the battle of Bicocca, Bandello was able to return to Milan, only to be forced into exile again four years later for reasons that remain obscure. What is certain, however, is that Bandello's possessions were sacked by Spanish soldiers in the service of Emperor Charles V, and that many of his books and papers were destroyed. Bandello chose at that point to turn "from Minerva to Mars," taking up arms for Federico Gonzaga, marquis of Mantova. During this time he would encounter Machiavelli and Giovanni delle Bande Nere. In 1528 he negotiated the marriage of Costanza Rangone to Cesare Fregoso, commander of the presidio of Verona, whom he accompanied to Verona the following year. After Fregoso was murdered in an ambush by agents of Charles V, Bandello became a servant and counsel to the widow Costanza, following her into exile first in Venice, and then in France. He became bishop of Agen, France where he died in 1561.

Bandello's *Novelle* numbered 214 stories in all, divided into four sections. The first three sections were published by the author in 1554, while the fourth was published posthumously in 1573. In his *Novelle,* Bandello mingled together stories about different topics, mixing comic stories with tragic stories, long stories with short, without regard to any unifying framework.

Bandello's story of "The Twins Nicuola and Paolo" and Shakespeare's *Twelfth Night* are both indebted to a play written in 1531 by the Sienese literary society, *Gl' Intronati,* entitled *Gl'Ingannati (The Deceived),* a Plautine comedy of deception and confused identity which, like Bandello's story, takes place against the back-drop of the sack of Rome. The story, "An Ass Tricks the Brothers of Modena," proves that one need not be a great genius to be a successful trickster, nor indeed is it necessary to be human. This story presents monastic life as only a Dominican like Bandello could. An "assinicide" is part of an elaborate deception by the buffoon Gonnella in "Gonnella Tricks Marquis Niccolo d'Este." No collection of comic stories from Bandello would be complete without one tale of the exploits of this his favorite fool. Marquis Niccolo (III) d'Este is here presented as a far more benevolent figure than would be expected of a man who ordered the beheading of his son and second wife.

🦁

Masuccio Salernitano was the pen name of Tomasso dei Guardati (1410?–1475?). Part of the Aragonese court of Naples, Masuccio was secretary to Roberto Sanseverino, the count of Marsico and grand admiral of the kingdom of Naples who was made prince of Salerno in 1463 by King Ferrante I. Little is known about Masuccio's personal life aside from his association with this court, but because of his *Il Novellino* he is regarded as a master of a grotesque style who was prone to moralizing digressions. Notorious for his anticlerical and misogynous tendencies, Masuccio dedicated his book to Ipolita D'Aragon e De' Visconti, duchess of Calabria, and he entitled it *Il Novellino* because of what he termed its "little merit." It was composed in five thematic sections of ten stories each.

In the first section, Masuccio was determined to "write with veracity" about the "wicked and depraved lives" of the false prophets. Written in indignant tones, these stories were dedicated to the highest nobles of Naples reflecting, according to Burckhardt, the anticlerical spirit of the Aragonese court.

The second section contains ten stories of "deception and harm received because of jealousy," various *facezie*, and stories "of other pleasing incidents without offense to anyone." Dedicated to Don Federico D'Aragon, this section contains the story of "Jealous Ioan Tornese" (11), and "How Saint Bernardine Was Tricked by Two Men from Salerno" (16). Saint Bernardine of Siena (1380–1444) was a popular preacher of the Franciscan order who vehemently denounced usury and the civil strife of his time. His many sermons were written with renowned freshness, energy of expression and clarity of thought. The story, "How Two Romans Deceived Sir Floriano of Bologna" (17), as well as an antecedent to Shakespeare's *Merchant of Venice* (14) are also found in this section.

Introducing the third section of *Il Novellino*, Masuccio describes his entry into "a secret and dreadful wood protected by knotty trunks and heavy thorns" wherein he encounters Mercury. The god elicits terror in the author by calling him by name, but seeing him burdened and confused, he shows him the way along the paths of Juvenal and Boccaccio. Masuccio's debt to Boccaccio has already been discussed, but here he also admits to emulating Juvenal (AD 60–130), whose ·Satires are an indictment of the immorality of his Roman world. Juvenal's lengthy sixth Satire, in fact, is an invective against the loose morals of women and, naturally enough, this third section contains the story, "How Viola Tried to Satisfy Her Three Lovers on the Same Night" (29). This story, which presents a rather bitter end for two of Viola's lovers, shares the central invention with one of Geoffrey Chaucer's Canterbury Tales, "The Miller's Tale."

The fourth section consists of tragic, passionate, and comic material mixed together so that "the horrid and sad are mixed with the facetious and ludicrous, in order that the sadness felt by the reader and listener may end in happiness." Here is related the story of "Two Dear Friends" (36), a trick turned upon itself wherein the deceivers are undone by their own maneuvers. The foiled plot ends, nevertheless, to the mutual delight of all concerned. Alongside this light-hearted story is a tragic version of the story of Romeo and Juliet.

The fifth and final section of Il Novellino recounts tales of great princes and a parliament in which Masuccio bitterly laments the death of Sanseverino.

🐦

Antonfrancesco Grazzini (1503–84) was esteemed for his lively and irreverent style of writing. He is best remembered for his collection of novelle, Le Cene or Dinner Parties. Begun as early as 1549, but not published until the eighteenth century, the Cene records the tales told by four young men and six young women who gathered for three parties on three separate evenings during winter. Ten stories are told during each of the three *Cene,* though only two stories, including that of "Doctor Manente," remain of the third and final *Cena.* The stories told during each succeeding *Cena* become progressively more complex, so that the stories of the final *Cena* "almost exceed the limits of the overall genre in their multiplicity of events and, in truth, foreshadow the novel of the seventeenth century."[19]

Grazzini was one of the founding members in 1540 of the *Accademia degli Umidi* (Academy of the Damp), named in praise of the creative powers of damp places. For his pen-name, he chose to call himself after one of the principle denizens of damp places, *Il Lasca,* the roach. This academy was the first such organization after the extinction of the Platonic Academy soon after Lorenzo de' Medici's death in 1492. Originally an informal fraternity of literary enthusiasts, Grazzini's academy gradually fell under the influence of pedants, creatures more horrid than any he might have imagined to exist in the verminous slime of his damp, generative world. In 1541 Duke Cosimo de' Medici professionalized the academy, giving it greater stature and importance. He charged its members with certain duties, such as public readings of translations from the classics, and changed its name to *Accademia Fiorentina.* Grazzini refused his duties, however, and publicly ridiculed the *Aramei,* a group of pedants who had infiltrated the academy. Headed by Pier Francesco Giambullari, canon of San Lorenzo, this group was called the *Aramei* because they traced the origins of the Florentine vernacular, not from Latin, but from a variant of Hebrew spoken in the region of Aram, which was believed to have been brought to Tuscany by the

Etruscans. Grazzini's derision of this notion won him a twenty-year expulsion from the academy. But Grazzini would have the last word. If Brunelleschi condemned the learned pronouncements of Gherardi da Prato and praised the dreams of "men without schooling," Grazzini wrote against pedants with unprecedented ferocity. In the second story of the first *Cene*, Grazzini recounts the tale of revenge against such a pedant, who is convinced to play a trick on an ill-mannered shop-keeper by urinating through an opening in the shop door. However, the trick is on him when inside the shop a trickster named Piloto pretends to be a cat and attacks and wounds the pedant's instrument.

It might be imagined that Grazzini's *Cene* would have found a wider audience had they not been so well-suited to the attention of censors. It is no surprise then that it was D. H. Lawrence, no stranger to censorship himself, who chose to introduce the English-speaking world to Grazzini with his translation of the story of "Doctor Manente" from the last *Cene*. Nevertheless, Grazzini's *novelle* were famous enough in Italy for the story of "A Trick Played by the Scheggia on Neri Chiaramontesi" to be adapted by the librettist Sem Benelli for Umberto Giordano's opera, *La Cena delle Beffe* (1909). But it is "The Trick Played by the Scheggia on Gian Simone Berrettaio" that has been called Grazzini's masterpiece, because it is so in keeping with his taste and comic spirit. This is the story in which the Scheggia and his companions, through a series of brilliant maneuvers, extort sufficient money from the hatter, Gian Simone, to pay for many delicious banquets.

Grazzini's pedant was indeed savaged by his deceivers, and some would say that even Gian Simone's treatment was unnecessarily cruel. But if we were to dismiss the deceived Gian Simone as vanquished by his loss, we would be far harsher to him than the Scheggia. Gian Simone was, after all, rich enough or fat enough or strong enough to be selected as a target, and when he eventually realized his folly, he was confronted with his own humanity. As D. H. Lawrence wrote in the introduction to his translation of Grazzini's "Doctor Manente":

> Nobody seems to have pitied the victim. [The victim] certainly never pitied himself; there is that to his credit vastly: when we think how a modern would howl to the world at large. No, they weren't sorry for themselves – they were tough without being hard-boiled. The courage of life is splendid in them. We badly need some of it today.

NOTES

1. Charles S. Singleton, "On Meaning in the *Decameron*," *Italica* 21 (1944): 117-24.

2. Millicent Joy Marcus, *An Allegory of Form: Literary Self-Consciousness in the Decameron* (Stanford French and Italian Studies 18, Anma Libri, 1979), p. 11.

3. See below, pp. xvi-xxi.

4. See below, pp. xxviii-xxxi.

5. See below, pp. xxvi-xxviii.

6. Analogous in tone to the Italian *novelle* although composed much earlier, were the French *fabliaux*, or comic verses, popular in the twelfth and thirteenth centuries. According to Donald R. Howard in his *Chaucer: His Life, His Works, His World* (New York: Fawcett Columbine, 1987), n. p. 416, "the *fabliaux* were popular tales of sex and revenge, having a set theme. They were French in origin, and were

in verse. Chaucer was probably following Boccaccio's lead in introducing them into his work, though Boccaccio had turned his fabliaux into prose." The Spanish picaresque novel later developed similarly realistic themes and colorful characters in the late sixteenth century.

7. Baldassare Castiglione, *The Book of the Courtier*, trans. George Bull (New York: Penguin, 1967), p. 155.

8. The beffa was also known in Italian as a *burla*, from which the word "burlesque" derives.

9. Jacob Burckhardt, *The Civilization of the Renaissance in Italy*, trans. S.G.C. Middlemore (Oxford & London: Phaidon, 1945), p. 98.

10. Antonio Manetti, *The Fat Woodworker*, trans. Robert L. Martone & Valerie Martone (New York: Italica Press, 1991).

11. Joan Gadol, *Leon Battista Alberti: Universal Man of the Renaissance* (Chicago: University of Chicago Press, 1969), p. 32.

12. See below, pp. xxiii-xxv.

13. For the Christian, Twelfth Night commemorates the arrival of the Magi in Bethlehem, but the Christian feast gradually "attracted to itself...a good deal of the license and even the specific customs of the pagan Saturnalia." See Anne Barton, "Introduction to Twelfth Night," in *The Riverside Shakespeare* (Boston: Houghton Mifflin, 1974), p. 404. The Saturnalia was the Roman year-end holiday beginning on December 17, in honor of the god of sowing and husbandry. During this holiday, the normal rules of social order were suspended: servants became masters and masters became servants, and a mock-kingship was won by casting lots. The revelry of Carnival, which extends from Epiphany (Jan. 6) to Ash Wednesday, may derive from the Saturnalia.

14. Geoffrey Bullough, *Narrative and Dramatic Sources of Shakespeare*, vol. 1 & 2 (New York: Routledge & Kegan Paul, 1957, 1958).

15. Frances A. Yates, *Theatre of the World* (Chicago: University of Chicago Press, 1969), p. 101.

16. Giovanni Gherardi da Prato, *Il Paradiso degli Alberti*, ed. by Antonio Lanza (Rome: Salerno, 1975), p. xlv.

17. Eugenio Battisti, Sonnet of Giovanni Gherardi da Prato to Filippo Brunelleschi and Brunelleschi's reply in *Filippo Brunelleschi, The Complete Work*, trans. by Robert Erich Wolf (New York: Rizzoli, 1981), pp. 323-24.

18. Hans Baron, *The Crisis of the Early Italian Renaissance* (Princeton: Princeton University Press, 1966), pp. 332-33.

19. R.J. Rodini, *Antonfrancesco Grazzini, Poet, Dramatist, and Novellieri* (Madison: University of Wisconsin Press, 1970), p. 151.

RENAISSANCE COMIC TALES

of Love, Treachery, and Revenge

⁂

MONTANINA'S DECEPTION

Gentile Sermini

𝕏

If only there were written records of the past, there's no doubt that people's memories of the past would be more perfect now, and they would remember things just as they once were. And so it won't be forgotten, I'd like to tell you a delightful little story that has just reached my ears.

In Perugia a young man from that city named Vannino, who was wealthy and loved by everyone, fell in love be-yond measure with a young woman whose name was Montanina. Montanina's husband, Andreoccio, was very jealous of her, and didn't stray far from her side either day or night. He never enjoyed going to vineyards or festivals without having her by his side. He abandoned his own affairs in order to protect her and look after her needs. The beautiful Montanina was very distressed by the jealous ways of her husband. As a wise woman it annoyed her chiefly because she knew she was so perfectly beautiful. Vannino, greatly enamored of her, often lingered around Montanina's house, even though he wasn't able to see very much of her thanks to the solicitous care of her jeal-ous husband. Still, he would see her once in a while – only for a flash – because she would flee in fear of Andreoccio, who was always threatening her in his contemptible way. This made Vannino desolate.

While still in the throes of his passion, Vannino met Mona Nuta, an ancient and skilled peddler. "Mona Nuta," he said, "I'd like you to sell some things that I have in my house."

She agreed, and the two of them set out for Vannino's house. When they arrived there and went inside Vannino said, "Here are the things that I want to sell. I've decided to trust you because you've always been affectionate and loving toward me and my family."

He made her promise to keep it a secret, and then the clever Nuta said, "I'll do whatever I can possibly do, within the bounds of decency."

Vannino responded, "You're the perfect friend without a doubt. Who would help me if you refused? It's important that you help me, since without you I can't do anything. My fate is in your hands. Now I'll see if our old friendship is worth anything."

Won over by his entreaties Nuta replied, "You know how to ask so well that I don't know how anyone could refuse you. I'll do whatever I can to help you."

"Granny, you'll be none the worse if you help me," Vannino said. "What I want from you is this." Unable to hold back a trickle of tears he quickly told her whom he was in love with and what he wanted her to do for him.

Mona Nuta, moved by pity for him, said, "Don't cry, son. I'll give you what you wish."

"Oh, but she has such a jealous husband," said Vannino, "that I don't know how you'll be able to speak to her."

Brave Nuta said, "Leave that for me to worry about. You make sure that I have a nice little coffer made of ivory and a pretty purse and leave it to me to do my best."

In no time Vannino found a good little coffer and a lovely and expensive purse and gave them to Nuta. He put two ducats in Nuta's hand pleading, "I don't want you to fail on your first try." She pretended not to want the money, pulling her hand away several times. Finally, acting as if she were being forced, she took it. Then she thanked him and left.

With the little coffer, the purse, and some others things that her trade required, she came to Andreoccio's house and went inside. Pretending not to know who lived there and pretending to be tired, she put all of her things down on the ground and sat down – almost lying down – on the bottom stair. Andreoccio wanted to go out, since he had kept guard over his wife all day, but the same thing happened to him as happens to the guard of a castle. After keeping a good watch all night, he abandons it momentarily at the precise moment when the enemy puts his ladders against the walls and conquers. So, as he came downstairs, he found Nuta lying at the bottom complaining that she was tired. He said to her, "What are you doing, Nuta?"

Cunning Nuta answered, " These packs have made me so tired that I can't go on anymore." Moaning she added, "I'll never have the heart to take them back home, and I'd be glad to meet a good and trustworthy person with whom I could leave them until tomorrow morning."

Simple Andreoccio said, "If you want to leave them here, throw them up to Montanina and she'll take care of them." He called, "Montanina, come here and chat with this peddler!"

Capricious Nuta said, "Don't rush me. I won't leave them with anyone I don't know."

Andreoccio went out saying, "I'll leave that worry with you."

Montanina, when she heard her name called, ran down-stairs and found Nuta looking very tired. She asked her what she was doing and Mona Nuta told her the same thing she had told Andreoccio. Montanina was moved to compassion and said, "Go along and rest yourself a little while."

Nuta, almost recovered, said, "God reward you, daughter." They climbed upstairs together and sat down. Montanina began to look over all the things for sale. She especially liked the coffer and the purse. Praising all of Mona Nuta's things, she asked the price of the coffer and the purse and also asked whom they had come from. Nuta answered her in a low voice saying, "These belonged to a young man, a very noble person in this city, and they are of great value." Lifting her eyes toward Montanina she said, "Ah, child, how beautiful you are! It's quite a pity that I hear your husband treats you so badly, since what he can do for you is not worth one of your nails. With your beauty and virtue you deserve to be the wife of an emperor, not that Andreoccio, but Fortune has willed that you should stay subject to this rogue. I grieve for you, unhappy woman! You have the person who first spoke of this marriage to blame. Your father would have done better to kill you with his own hands than to give his consent. But since it's done, one must make the least wicked of painful choices. My daughter, I have compassion for only two people: one is you, the other is my neighbor, a rich young man who's handsome, delightful, decent, from a good family, bold, and most courteous. I understand that he is so much in love that he has forgotten everything else and is ready to die. I see him consuming his wealth, since he pays no attention to maintaining it. He thinks only of pleasing the one who so pleases him. No one but me knows the name of the person he loves.

"I know because one day when I went to see about some things, he met me, and I showed him this coffer and this purse. He wanted to buy them and asked how much I wanted for them. When he paid me he asked, 'Do you have any pretty rings or bracelets? Let me know since I won't consider how much they cost as long as they are very pretty.' It was then that I thought he might be in love. I said to him, 'You don't have a wife or any sisters who are getting married. Why do you want to buy these things? What do you want to do with them? The only reason is love! For pity's sake, tell me the truth, are you in love?' At this point he began to weep and could say nothing. This made everything clear. I felt great compassion for him, considering his youth, shyness, and modesty, and once more I asked him if he might be in love. I pressured him to confess to me and tell me who she was and if he would tell me, I would give him the most beautiful jewels for her hands. Sighing deeply he said in a trembling voice, 'Get them.' I replied that he would never have them if he did not confess the truth to me.

"He admitted that he was in love but he would not say with whom. So I said to him, 'My son, who would you confide in if not in me, since you know perfectly well that

I was born and raised in your house? Perhaps I can give you some advice.' I also swore that I would never say anything. Finally, with tears, he confided in me, but he pleaded and threatened to kill me if he ever heard anything back. He gave me these little things so that I could bring them on his behalf to the person he named. Moved by compassion, I decided to help him as much as I possibly could. Now if you want to know who sent them, and who they are for, please ask me."

After she heard this story, Montanina felt great pity for the youth. She still didn't know who he might be, and it seemed to her that it would be a thousand years before she would hear the name of this graceful woman whom Vannino loved so much. She begged Mona Nuta to tell her, and clever Nuta said, "Tell me, my daughter, since you are blessed, what woman could be so ruthless and cruel, that if she knew a man loved her so much, she wouldn't feel compassion when she saw such a young pilgrim ready to die for her?"

"Certainly," said Montanina, won by mercy, "she her-self shouldn't live."

Nuta said, "Oh, how well you speak, daughter! Now I want to tell you. The beloved is *you,* and the lover is Vannino, and therefore this coffer is yours, and also the purse. I have brought them to you on his behalf."

Not thinking of herself and feeling only pity, Montanina listened carefully to that woman. Then, in the instant she heard all this she opened her eyes and grew pale, almost unable to answer, and in anguish said, "Don't say these things to me. I don't want to hear them." But in her heart, once she had heard that woman's message and knew that Vannino longed for her, she didn't turn against her lover, since Venus would not allow her to be spared the experience of being loved. And so, in Montanina's secret heart, her love for Vannino grew, although she didn't want to reveal it to Nuta.

Shrewd Nuta saw and heard Montanina's reply and said, "Daughter, I don't speak to you with rudeness, nor would Vannino wish me to disgrace you with what I say. But I firmly believe that you need to accept these gifts and agree to listen to some words that will both preserve your honor and save his life. I won't tell anyone about you, and I want you to rest assured that I don't advocate any indecent risk to your body. Choose the time and the place that he can speak to you forthrightly and he will. Don't think that I would propose anything else to you, since you swear by your honesty with one hand, but I swear with two. Now tell me, dear, what time should he come and where should he meet you?"

Montanina, of two opposing minds, struggled with herself and didn't answer. On the one hand she wanted to hear what he had to say, but on the other she didn't know how this would be possible because of her jealous husband. As she thought the whole thing over she became somewhat overwhelmed by Nuta's arguments. She finally answered, "Mona Nuta, you have said so many things that I feel overcome and don't know how to answer you, but I say this: Take away the coffer and the purse since if I keep them in the house and Andreoccio sees them, he'll surely slash my veins. This would certainly not please Vannino. And as for listening to what Vannino has to say, I don't see how, since Andreoccio never leaves the house."

Nuta said, "We'll find a way around that."

After they discussed it for a while Montanina said, "If that happens I'll be able to listen to what he wants to tell me. But if Andreoccio doesn't leave the city I wouldn't dare."

Nuta said, "Will you give me your word on this if Andreoccio does leave the city?"

"Yes," said Montanina, swearing to Nuta. Then Nuta left, thanking Montanina, and she carried off the gifts so no one would see them.

Vannino was hiding outside waiting to catch Nuta as soon as she came out the front door. He went right up to her and asked, "Have we got good news?" Cheerfully she answered him that yes, they did, and together the two went to Vannino's house to sit down, so that Nuta could recount the whole story to him in detail. His joy was beyond all measure. Then Nuta said, "Vannino, things are going well. I know that Marino, your dear friend, is one of the priors. Go to him and suggest some pretense for Andreoccio to leave Perugia for a few days, otherwise you won't be able to build your little nest. Once this is done, things will begin to proceed as they should."

This idea cheered Vannino, who uttered his thanks and left for Marino's palace. Since Marino knew all of Vannino's secrets, especially this one, Marino said, "I'll help you. Go now and come back to me this evening, because by then I'll have made all the arrangements with my partners to send Andreoccio out of town as far as Assisi on a small matter concerning the Commune." So, with everything settled, Vannino left, and Marino spent some time with his colleagues so that in the end it was left to him to send whomever he wanted to Assisi. Immediately Marino sent for Andreoccio, who quickly came.

Acting very friendly Marino brought him into a room and made him sit next to him, pretending that he wanted his help. He said, "I'm glad you're here, Andreoccio. The reason that I've sent for you is this: we have to send a messenger to Assisi to take care of something. It was left for me to choose someone to send, and I'd like to ask you to go, because I want the matter to be handled quietly. I've always felt great affection for you, and since you've never held any office in the Commune, I've decided that you can begin to have some responsibility and have this honor that will benefit you. To begin with, I will give you as much work as possible. Therefore, be ready to-morrow night with two horses and come to see me at eleven o'clock, and I'll give you instructions for what you'll have to do. Because it's important, we want you to leave tomorrow night so no one will be suspicious. Also, please don't speak of this matter to anyone or tell anyone that you are on a mission for us. Say that you're going for your own business. So, make your arrangements and return to me at the time we've set."

Andreoccio recognized Marino's great love for him, and so he thanked him and accepted the mission. He left him saying that he would get himself ready secretly and return to get the instructions at eleven o'clock, then he would leave with the work that he was being secretly sent to do. Although he promised to carry out the matter in secret, he was so overjoyed to be the ambassador that it made him forget his promise. He left the palace flushed and breathless, walking quickly down the street, and full of pride that he was going as an ambassador to Assisi, he told his secret to everyone he met. When he reached his own house he told Montanina all about it, but he told her not to tell anyone. Andreoccio's profound sense of judgment and obedience made him tell her this, since he was ordered by Marino to keep it a secret. Though the matter was so unimportant that the house cook could just as easily have been sent, Andreoccio would have done the same thing whether the matter was great or small. As it was, if he had known why he was going to Assisi, he would have told it to everyone and asked them all to keep it a secret.

The next evening Andreoccio went back to Marino's at eleven o'clock, as arranged, to receive his instructions. Then he thanked Marino and left. He raced so quickly to his own house that he couldn't have better betrayed his business than by his quick step, flushed face, and preoccupied expression. When he reached his house, all out of breath, he asked Montanina to get the things ready that he needed for his trip.

As the bells for penance were rung, he mounted his horse and left with his servant, but before he left he gave Montanina all the details at length saying, "I think I'll be away for three days. Stay away from the window and remain inside the house with the front door locked until I return home." While she promised to do so she wisely begged him with tearful eyes to return to her as soon as possible. She also showed him in other ways that it was going to be very sad for her to be without him for the three days he said he would have to be away. Like the wise woman she was, she pretended not to know anything about his journey. But she understood everything, and it seemed a thousand years before he would go, though she pretended just the opposite. In the end, Andreoccio departed on horseback riding through the public square – where Marino had forbidden him to go – so that he would be well seen by all. But he went as he pleased, reveling in the glory of being seen rather than keeping his business a secret, as he made his way toward Assisi.

Meanwhile Vannino had quickly learned about Andreoccio's mission from Marino. Together they discussed what they would now do. With everything arranged by Marino, Vannino went to meet with Nuta and advise her of everything. Nuta didn't rest but, as her craft required, went to Montanina's house with certain articles of clothing and other little things on hand to sell. There she was greeted with a much more amiable and pleasant welcome than she had received the first time. She said to Montanina, "Daughter, out of pity for so rare a pilgrim, who is pining away to death, I return to you, since God well knows that it's because of his suffering that I've come to you.

"Now tell me, daughter, it seems that Andreoccio has to leave Perugia for a few days tomorrow evening. You know what you've promised me. I've come to rescue that young man who loves you so much. By God, you can save his life. Now you can offer a reason for him to live or die, as you wish. I've promised him, on your behalf, that you'll listen to what he has to say tomorrow evening. Since he doesn't want anything except to speak with you honestly, he is looking forward to this with great joy. If this proves hopeless, he would kill himself at your front door, and you would become disgraced and bear the sin and shame of it. But now you can solve this with your decency. You're young. Pay attention to my advice, since you know I wish you well. Rest assured that if I believed that this would result in any damage to your honor or any offense to God I would sooner kill myself with my own hand. To tell you the truth, I want nothing but to keep my promise to Vannino, and so what I do is with compassion for him and honor for you.

"Finally, I want you to know that tomorrow evening, he will steal into the garden behind your house at three o'clock. At that time you should go to your bedroom window that opens onto the garden a little above the ground. He'll go there and speak with you at the window. I'm sure he won't demand more of your honor, and, as for what he'll tell you, you'll be able to answer him as a lady. And don't think that I would want you to allow him to come into the house for anything, since if I didn't trust him, daughter, you wouldn't forgive me, and I couldn't give my word. I've already lived honorably for seventy years and I wouldn't want to lose what honor I've had until now."

"Now this is what you should do: When you hear the hour strike three tomorrow night, after that wicked Andreoccio has left, go quietly down to that window where Vannino will be able to talk to you. Be sure that the front door is securely locked to eliminate any risk. Now, I don't want to stay any longer since Vannino is waiting for me. I'll see how wise you are and if you want him dead or alive."

Montanina considered what Nuta had said; first, the problems with her husband, then Vannino's love for her. She was moved to compassion for Vannino because of Nuta's words, and she preferred to save him rather than behave mercilessly. Wisely she answered, "Mona Nuta, you tell me things that I know very well aren't true. Still, so that a bigger scandal won't ensue from this, so that he won't kill himself on my door-step, and because of the promise you said you made to him, and to prevent any shame on my part, I agree to allow him to steal into the garden. At three o'clock I'll be at that window, after I've made sure that all the doors of the house are securely locked." And she concluded: "Mona Nuta, I know that you care about my honor and will therefore guide this matter to a good and just conclusion."

Mona Nuta embraced Montanina saying, "My child, you have charmed me with your wisdom, honesty, and discretion. Now leave it to me to manage things so that both you and he will be left content, preserving your honor with everything kept confidential. Now go, blessed one – since I want to comfort your servant who loves you so much – and do as we've arranged. Be sure, however, that you have everything clear in your own mind."

Then Nuta departed and went quickly to Vannino, who was waiting for her. With great joy she told him everything and he thanked her with all his heart. Then he went to see Marino at the palace, to tell him what had happened. Together Marino and Vannino gave the orders for the evening's plan. Armed with swords, they left the palace a little before three o'clock, taking along a small ladder to put under the window where Montanina was sure to be waiting, as Nuta suggested. When they arrived and entered the garden Marino hid under a little bower while Vannino put the ladder beside the small window so that he could climb inside to Montanina. They waited until the bells for three rang. Montanina waited fearlessly for her lover with great longing and when she heard the bells ring three o'clock she quickly went downstairs and ran to the open window, leaning out to see if Vannino was down below.

Vannino didn't hesitate, but quickly and closely embraced Montanina saying, "My lady, greetings!"

Then she started to get frightened and said, "Vannino, get down on the ground and say what you want."

Vannino said, "Oh my hope, oh I love you more than any other being, oh I wish you a thousand times more honor than I wish for myself, for God's sake hear what I have to say. I've been chased here by the family of the Podesta, and I'm certain that they're lurking nearby. I had to enter the garden without letting them see me. But they can see me up here from the street. For God's honor, as well as yours and mine, let me come inside your room. I'm not lying to you. Trust me and let's shield our honor now."

When wise Montanina heard this she, of course, wanted the same thing, but for the sake of her purity she pretended she didn't understand him and said, "If this is true, I will preserve our honor on the condition that you promise me, upon your faith, that you will not taint me or my honor in any way." Vannino promised and swore to it. Then she let him come inside her room. But once inside, he quickly forgot his promise and flung his arms around her neck, kissing her lovingly, hoping for the emotional response that he longed for.

Brave Montanina understood the situation and said, "Vannino, I beg you, since you have more to learn about me and because we have been brought to this, don't pluck the flower hastily when, with more leisure, you'll be able to eat the entire fruit."

Vannino, seeing that he was welcomed without great protest but with discretion, decided to go along with her and expecting that he would later be welcomed again, said, "My lady, I'll be satisfied with whatever pleases you." And after a delightful kiss he left her alone.

Montanina had already guessed what she would need, and a supper was prepared for her and for her companion. She said to Vannino, "You say you want to speak to me. Let's go up to my bedroom so that we won't be disturbed, and there you can say what you must and what you please." And so together they climbed the stairs and went into the beautiful bedroom where there was a good fire and a little round table set with a delicate dinner. Montanina said, "I was ready to sit down at this table, but waited a little while for something and, in the meantime, heard the bell ring three. I remembered what I had promised Mona Nuta, and thinking that you would not stay long, I left the table and everything as you see here and ran downstairs to see if you were coming. Now the dinner is still here. Perhaps you haven't had supper, so let's wash our hands and then you can dine with me. Even though this is so unexpected, I couldn't be more pleased. And you, obviously a wise man, will accept my apology for not having foreseen this."

Vannino took delight in all this and felt like he was entering a new paradise. He said, "My lady, you've provided twice as much as I deserve, especially being here with you, and in this pleasant and noble setting that you have arranged. If I was a true servant before, I now rightly call myself a slave, not only your slave, but your slave's slave, and I graciously accept your invitation." So together they washed their hands and sat down at the table

near the fire where they enjoyed their dinner with pleasant conversation, remembering lost times, one talking of
one thing and the other of another, saying, "then you did
this and you did that."

"Do you remember that feast of Saint Ercolano when
you never even looked toward me?" Vannino asked.

"I saw you quite well with my eyes covered, but while
you were in the piazza jousting you didn't hear of my
compassion and deep sorrow for you when you were
thrown off your mount and dragged by your horse. I
feared you might be dead. God knows the pain that I felt
from it, seeing that you would not come back to me for
quite some time."

"And when you stood up at the window when I entered the piazza in armor, if you had given me the
slightest sign I would have conquered every knight that
day and you would have reviled me for it! But do you
know what I say? You have never done any harm to me
that I couldn't repay."

"Me, what have I done to you? It wouldn't be fair if I
didn't defend myself from your advances. You can be
sure, Vannino, that the reason for much of my behavior
was my fear of Andreoccio."

"I always knew that, but in spite of him I'm here anyway. Oh, if he knew about this what he would say? He
ordered you to lock all the doors securely."

"Well, I obeyed him, but he didn't say anything about
the window, and if he had, you wouldn't be here now.
Nevertheless you've come and you're inside my house; I
don't intend to treat you with anything but kindness. The
only reason I let you come inside was because you were

afraid that the family of the Podesta would see you up on that ladder."

Vannino answered meekly saying, "My lady, if I have failed at anything, blame it on Venus, not on me." And exchanging these and other pleasantries they finished their supper.

Later when they rose from the table they sat closer together and redoubled their banter until they were tired of talking and became sleepy. Then each one rose to avenge the injuries they received and, setting out for the bed, they began to undress with great joy. They forgot their discussions, and Montanina took her place first, but before Vannino could take his Andreoccio returned.

While he was riding on his horse it started to rain. Andreoccio wasn't able to navigate a small ditch, and his horse fell. Andreoccio would have been in danger of drowning if not for the quick help of his servant and, when he was pulled from the ditch he saw that the water level didn't subside but continued to rise. Since he wasn't a brave person, he decided to return to Perugia, intending to ride out again later in the day, even though this would not agree with the prior's instructions. So he turned around and rode back to Perugia where he found the gates of the city unlocked. When he reached his house he and his servant dismounted quickly and knocked at the door and called out.

All of a sudden Vannino and Montanina heard the voice and knew it was Andreoccio. Upstairs each one felt such dreadful sorrow that neither the heart nor the pen could bear to describe it; only the heart could understand it. Montanina felt such a painful blow that it almost vanquished her. I don't dare say anything about Vannino. He saw the danger and quickly dressed, wrapping his cloak around his arm and picking up his sword. Brave Montanina, wise and prudent, realized what the situation was and decided to cover for herself and Vannino. First, she took a medicinal drink that she kept hidden in the house for other purposes. Then she said to Vannino, "Climb inside this chest, safe and secure, and don't make a sound. I faithfully promise you that before long I'll restore you to a position that will please you. What he does to us now we'll soon do to him in a way that will vex him. Don't give it a thought, dear heart. Climb in and believe me."

Vannino decided to entrust his fate to her and so he climbed into the large chest where she kept her precious things. With his sword and some jam for comfort he would endure it. And so, locking him inside the large chest with the key hidden in the lining of her sleeve, Montanina went to the window, and in a small and apprehensive voice she asked, "Who's that knocking?"

To this Andreoccio and his servant said, "It's Andreoccio."

She went downstairs and opened the doors saying, "God forgive you, Andreoccio."

He wanted to embrace her after he had suffered so much, but he saw her looking very pained and said, "What's wrong with you?"

She answered in a labored voice, "I was asleep, feeling sorry for you because of the terrible rain. I was afraid that something might happen to you, especially at night, and I dreamed that the water took you away. In the middle of my worry I heard you knock on the door, and recognizing the servant's voice, I said, 'Alas, my sweet husband has drowned. Here is the servant who brings me the bad news.' That's the reason why I've come in such a terrible state. I can't put aside the pain I felt. And still I prayed to God that our deaf maid would hear him and answer the door, but it was no use, and then I heard your voice. Then I felt consoled and I forced myself to come downstairs and that's why I look like I've suffered so much." She then embraced him saying, "Welcome back! To think that I believed I'd never touch you or see you again and now I can see and touch you, praise God! You know what I say to you, Andreoccio? If you don't help me, I won't be able to climb these stairs."

Leaning on him she climbed the stairs and went into the bedroom. Andreoccio felt that he was to blame, so he held his tongue. And although he was still soaking wet, muddy, tired, and needing rest, he tried to comfort Montanina, describing the danger he faced, and apologizing for having to turn around. While he spoke the medicine did its work. Montanina felt its effect and it caused her to faint. There was little he could do to help her recover and so, while she lamented, Andreoccio put her to bed. She moaned continuously, feeling herself fail little by little, and because her pulsing veins were continuously contracting and slowing, she asked for the priest and two friars of Saint Dominic, and also the notary so she could make out her last will and testament.

Andreoccio called in the neighbors to stay by her side, and they surrounded her to comfort her as best they could, but no comfort helped. She asked again for the friars and the notary, and Andreoccio realized that he should call them to his house. The friars came because they realized they were needed, and they began to read the last rites of the soul.

Then Montanina recovered her voice a bit and recognizing the friars and Ser Alberto she said, "Praise God. I want to make out my will and testament."

The notary saw his cue and brought in the necessary witnesses saying, "My lady, say what you please."

She called Andreoccio and said, "Stay to listen, and likewise you, friars, and also the witnesses." First she said, "I bequeath my body to Saint Dominic, to be put into the sepulcher of Andreoccio, and I leave every part of my dowry, with everything that I possess, to my husband Andreoccio. I do this on the condition that I can depend on him and upon the deeds he will do for my soul, and with the understanding that, in the memory of my dear and blessed sister, certain little things that I've affection-ately always kept by me, should remain near me now, at my death. These things are in that chest at the foot of the bed. With this I will die content, and to be certain of this I beg you, Andreoccio, that you will allow it."

He agreed to do what she asked. Then she said, "Sir Alberto, draw up the will as I've said. I want to make it clear that this chest is to be guarded continuously by these friars and when I am carried out for burial, I want the chest to be kept close to my body while it is carried to the grave, so that nothing is touched. I want this chest buried with me." And she turned to the friars and said, "You will be guardians of the chest, and if it is ever opened or touched, except as I've specified, Andreoccio will have nothing of mine. If you carry out my will regarding the chest, I'd be pleased for it to be my gift to the two of you. But if you don't do what I've said, I'll leave my gift to the

Monastery of St. Dominic. My last will is that you friars will be guardians of this chest." They promised that they would do this and Andreoccio was in complete agreement. Sir Alberto drew up the will. With an eye to her own health or Vannino's, who was being tortured inside the chest, Montanina sent Andreoccio and the others away, and she called Friar Ramondo to hear her confession. He went to her side and she confessed a few sins, then slowly told him, "I beg you and Friar Giovanni, who is here with you, to say fifty masses for my soul. Promise me this. I want all the things that are in this chest to be yours alone. They are worth 200 ducats. Tell me if you don't want it so I can arrange for someone else to take care of it." The two friars were not slow, and both approached her and promised her, on their word, to do it. With this understanding Montanina continued, "So that the others won't take it away before you, I want you to swear to me that tonight, when all the other friars are asleep, you'll both come here together with an iron rod to lift the stone, and a pair of tongs, a hammer and a little miter to pull the lock out of the chest. Take the things inside the chest and divide them between you, since I've given them to you. Otherwise, if you don't take it tonight as you've promised, I want it to go to the monastery. I leave this up to you."

The friars promised her and swore upon their hearts to do exactly as she had asked, saying, "We'll bring the rod and other things that we'll need to open it. And since your sepulcher is outside the church, we'll arrange a way to leave. God will reward your soul for this charity, since God knows our needs." Then Friar Ramondo gave her absolution. She began to fail seriously and to moan while the opium took its course. Her veins began to close again and her pulse faded, and in a little while she drew her last breath. Andreoccio and all the others wailed loudly.

Vannino, inside the chest, heard her last words and the promises made by the friars because Montanina spoke loud enough on purpose so that he would hear. He took great comfort from her words, saying to himself, "I'll get out of here if they open the tomb and the chest." He knew she wasn't dead, and this made him quite happy since he knew he would soon be with her. He decided to allow himself to be buried inside the chest, and making the best of the situation, he concentrated on getting some rest. The friars never abandoned the chest, concerned more about the treasure inside it than about carrying out her will.

In the meantime, Andreoccio, without going into the specific details, made all the necessary arrangements. The hour of the burial arrived, near vespers, and people began to gather to pay their last respects until almost all of Perugia was there. When the time came to bring out the body, it was carried from Andreoccio's house high upon a bier followed by the great chest, which was carried high on the shoulders of four friars of St. Dominic. If, at first, the people grieved and wept when they saw the coffin, when they saw the chest come into view all of a sudden they began to grin, unable to hold back their laughter. Everyone was astonished since they didn't know what to make of the chest.

Since the people of Perugia generally appreciate something amusing, there wasn't one person there who wouldn't have laughed when he heard the jokes and retorts that were exchanged.

One said, "Listen here. This is a very strange custom. You always see them carrying the chest when a girl marries a husband and moves her bags and dowry into the husband's house, but not when she's taken to the grave."

Another said, "Hey, you don't know what's inside! Oh, the devil! Don't you see that Andreoccio is sending his furniture on since he'll be sent to the otherworld this year!"

"Hey, look," said another to those friars carrying it, "Do you friars want some more weight to carry? Tell me the truth, does it weigh a lot?"

"Try carrying it for a little while yourself, and you'll know, by God. It feels like a slab of marble with a steel covering. I think the devil's inside."

Another friar said, "This devil has broken my bones. I say we throw it down and kill him!"

The other answered, "What a good-for-nothing load this is."

Then the two friars who were supposed to be guarding the chest and pretending to say their offices said to one another, "Yes for you this load is good-for-nothing," since they were waiting for the stuff that was inside the chest.

Another said, "Listen here, would you sell that chest? What price would you take for it?"

And another, "You carry chests well, but you're not worthy to carry your tonsure. What would a hundred chests of this rubbish be worth? How would anyone know what's inside that you rascal friars are carrying off? Have you robbed Andreoccio's house? Isn't the body enough? Have you also taken the plates and the crockery?"

The women came to the windows calling to one another, each one grieving for Montanina's death, but still laughing and bantering in surprise at the chest. Some boys gathered and began to shout, "Stone them! Stone them! These traitorous friars are carrying away both the people and their belongings! If you don't drop the chest to the ground we'll pelt you with stones."

If at first the people laughed, now they doubled over with laughter and banter, and pretending to warn and upbraid those boys they encouraged them. They signaled to them that they could do what they were threatening without fear of any consequence. The boys' confidence grew, and they began to toss stones and mud at the friars who carried the chest. The other friars couldn't restrain their laughter. The boys chased them, shouting together, "Throw it down." Since the boys threw a continuous rain of stones at the friars, the four who were carrying the chest couldn't dodge them and began to lose their grip. When the friars were pretty well beaten and full of mud, another clod of mud hit one of them in the face, covering it completely. He was in so much pain that he let go of the chest and ran away.

With all the pain he was suffering, Vannino encased inside couldn't restrain himself any longer and shouted in a disguised voice, "What the devil are you doing to me?" At this point, the three other friars who were trying to hold onto the chest called the others for help, but when they heard the voice from inside the chest they suddenly became terrified and, afraid that there might be evil spirits inside, dropped it. Then the boys chased the friars with stones all the way to Saint Dominic's, so that everyone laughed even harder. Things seemed bad to Vannino. The

funeral procession had stopped and there was no one who
would pick up the chest. Every single friar avoided it,
except the two friars charged with guarding it. For them
avarice conquered fear. They offered to carry it themselves and it was placed on their shoulders. If at first it
seemed heavy for four people, I don't think it seemed
light for two, but their desire for what was inside gave
them their strength. And so both the coffin and the chest
moved off and in a short time they arrived at St.
Dominic's where the funeral rites were performed. The
coffin and the chest were taken outside, and the friars
buried Montanina in Andreoccio's tomb, placing the chest
beside her. At first, though, there was another great battle
with the boys who didn't want to let the chest be buried,
and so the friars again felt a rain of stones.

After the stone slab was turned and the tomb was covered, the friars made a hasty departure since they were actually chased back home by the boys' stones. Andreoccio
and the people had already gone to his house, and while
he wept continuously he received everyone's condolences
one more time before they left him. So Andreoccio stayed
inside his house, and the boys, unable to do anything else
to the friars, went on their way. Thanks to this, all of
Perugia, men, women, and children remained in a festive
mood for a good month. With a lot of joking, they talked
of nothing else.

The story of the death of Montanina is plain for all to
see. Her widower, Andreoccio, remained tearful and sad.
And if Vannino was slow to pick the first flower, his
example of how to wait patiently for the whole bunch
should serve other young men who find themselves in
similar situations. If they don't want to end up encased

like him, it's better to have the egg today than to have
the hen tomorrow.

꿹

So Vannino was in the chest near Montanina who lay
entombed while the opium ran its course. And, since this
drug had never harmed anyone, by ten o'clock she
revived. When she woke and realized where she was, she
called Vannino in a soft voice. At first he was a little
frightened, but then he clearly recognized Montanina's
voice and was cheered up. He replied, "My lady, what do
you want?"

She said, "Just remember that I'm alive and well, and
don't be afraid. Before long we'll be out of this place."

No need to say that Vannino was overjoyed, because
that's obvious. But he told her how he was doing and
they rejoiced in soft voices without being able to touch or
see one another.

Then Montanina said, "Vannino, I've given a lot of
thought to our escape so that you and I will be safe and
easily able to recover our lost dowries."

Vannino answered with joy, "Earlier I had decided that
I'd rather die inside here than disgrace you. Now I'm
happier than I've ever been."

So together the two of them discussed how they would
escape to safety. They talked cheerfully and pleasantly in
this way until six o'clock. At the appointed hour, Friar
Ramondo and Friar Giovanni arrived with pliers,
hammers, wedges, and a large pole. Prying the stone slab
off the tomb with the pole, one of them sat astride the
rim of the sepulcher from outside while the other took the
pliers and other tools and perched on the edge of it in

order to pull out the chest's lock. As they had arranged, Vannino and Montanina quietly waited for the time when they could leave. It seemed like a thousand years before the lid was finally opened. The solicitous and avaricious friars exerted themselves, pried open the lock, and opened the lid of the chest to take the treasure inside. Vannino was poised with sword in hand and suddenly stood up. Then, with a terrifying shriek, he leapt out of the chest and quickly chased them away.

Since they believed that Vannino was an evil spirit, the friars were so bewildered and frightened that they fled. Vannino picked up their tools and hurled them after them, following them for a little way and shouting. They lost their wits and raced back to their cells where Friar Giovanni died of fear that same night. Friar Ramondo went mad and never regained his senses. This is the fate the two friars earned for themselves.

As soon as the two friars were gone, Vannino and Montanina left the grave, took everything out of the chest and went to Vannino's house. After enjoying a good breakfast, which they needed, they went off to bed without being hampered by Andreoccio. With great happiness they lovingly set out to retrieve their lost dowries. I won't bother to write about the joy and happiness that they shared because anyone with sense would know all about it. In pleasure they hid for ten days and then, in total agreement, they decided to live together for the rest of their lives.

To do things properly they decided that Vannino would act as if he were suffering over the death of his lover and he would stay alone at home in deep grief. He would tell his relatives that he wanted to spend the rest of his troubled life in another land because he could not bear to live in Perugia, where the woman he loved so much had died. He gave the order for his housekeeper to pack up his house and his possessions, and he arranged to go to Lombardy. Vannino left with Montanina disguised as a servant. Riding on horseback they arrived quickly at the magnificent city of Milan, and there they took a house for two years, where they lived in joy, festivity, and mirth.

After the two years, they decided to return to Perugia. Montanina had studied the Milanese speech during those two years so that she would not be known in Perugia or even in Milan itself as anything other than Milanese. Then, Vannino wrote a letter to his relatives, delighting to tell them about the woman he had married in Milan. She was a Milanese named Pellegrina, the daughter of a gentleman, Giovagnuolo de' Rusconi, who was a courtier of the most illustrious Duke of Milan. He had died three years ago, and Pellegrina was raised by a friend who treated her as his own daughter, since she had neither father nor mother.

Vannino wrote in his letter how he had first decided not to marry, since he felt like the widower of Montanina, but one fine day at a tournament in Milan, many of the most noble women came to see the joust, and she was among them. She hesitated a little, turning to her companions with a gentle gesture, and then, as Fortune pleased, she turned her face toward him, and it seemed that he was seeing the graceful figure and angelic face of Montanina. If he was not so sure that she was already dead and buried, he would have truly believed that she was Montanina. As soon as he saw her, out of love for the woman she resembled, he fell in love with her just as he had fallen in love with Montanina. And when he learned who she was, and whose daughter she was, he changed his mind about never wanting to marry, and he firmly decided, if it were possible, to marry her. He then became friendly with a courtier who was a great friend of this woman's father so that he would be the go-between, and so he could get to know her better. Now, compelled by his love for his native land, he decided to return to Perugia, and he would be there soon, and in time he'd let them know when so that they would see to it that his new bride would be honored upon her arrival.

The letter reached Perugia and the news spread quickly around the city that Vannino had married a Milanese woman who resembled Montanina and that he would soon return to Perugia. After Vannino wrote, he was encouraged by the letters he got in return from his relatives and so he prepared to leave. Montanina was rebaptized Pellegrina and took two new attendants who were unaware of her real name and believed that she was Milanese, as they heard in the house, and that she was the daughter of Giovagnuolo de' Rusconi. Thus they set off, and in a few days reached Panigale, near Perugia, where Vannino owned some land. From there he sent one of his messengers to Perugia to let his relatives know that he was in Panigale. He sent word that he would be in Perugia the next day and he wanted them to meet him and arrange a dinner. The relatives received the letter in celebration and arranged for everything that they needed.

At the agreed time outside the city gate, relatives and friends greeted Vannino on horseback. After numerous embraces, in a family-like gathering, they all entered Perugia in a throng. Vannino's return was known throughout the city and many people waited for him in the streets. Among them, by chance, was Andreoccio. Vannino entered the city with a happy face, and everyone welcomed him. Andreoccio greeted him and his wife as the others had done, while Vannino and his wife returned the courteous greeting, just they had to the others, and then rode to Vannino's house. When she saw Andreoccio, her true husband, Pellegrina acted as if she had never seen him before, and when she passed by, everyone said of her, "That woman looks just like Montanina."

Since the story had spread throughout Perugia that Vannino had married a woman who closely resembled Montanina, and that he had married her because of this resemblance, every person believed that it was true, just as she and Vannino wanted. When they arrived at Vannino's house her sweet actions showed that she did not recognize it and she pretended to believe that they had farther to go. When she saw that the others had dismounted, she turned back toward Vannino with a timid and modest demeanor, almost asking if she would have to dismount here. Then all the youths dismounted, and with gestures and words they showed her that she had to dismount, and they offered to help her. She also saw that Vannino was already on the ground, and he motioned to her to join him. She put her hands on the saddle and told the person who was offering to help her to stand aside. She took a jump, just like a good squire would do, and got down from her horse where she was welcomed by the women who waited for her.

Then everyone went into the dining hall and again they were welcomed with great joy. After a good meal, with even more young women in attendance, Montanina took a little nap in the bedroom. When the dinner hour came, since the house was already well supplied, they washed their hands, sat down at the table, and dined honorably. Whenever her companions spoke to her, Pellegrina always responded in the Lombard speech. All the men and women said to one another, "Vannino is very lucky since he could not have done better than to chance upon his every desire! That woman is beautiful, wise, honest, and virtuous, and she is exactly like the woman whom he loved so much. If she had not already died more than two years ago I would be suspicious that she was really Montanina." Everyone at the dinner said this, and although she was well aware of whom they were talking about, she pretended not to understand anything she heard, concentrating instead on dining and honoring the person by her side. In this way, she won everyone's good will. Dinner ended with songs, dances, and music while everyone lingered a little while longer. Finally the entire group went away to rest, even Vannino and Pellegrina.

The story of their marriage spread quickly through all Perugia. They lived together fourteen years, and there never was a person who would know her identity for certain, except her mother. And so it happened that Montanina was moved by tenderness to compassion for her mother, who believed her daughter, Montanina, was dead. One morning, her mother encountered her, and since she seemed to be her daughter, she began to weep out of love for her.

Montanina couldn't bear for her mother to suffer such pain, so when she went home she said to Vannino, "I'm happy to hide from everyone, except my dear mother." He agreed and secretly arranged, under false pretenses, for

Montanina to bring her mother inside her house. The mother came, and she and the daughter sat together in the bedroom. Montanina knelt down at her mother's feet, telling her, "If you promise me and swear to keep secret what I tell you, I promise to tell you the greatest story, and you'll be more grateful about it than you've ever been about anything you've ever heard." Her mother stared at her as she spoke, since she appeared to be exactly like her daughter. Since she wanted to hear what the young woman had to say she promised and swore never to speak of it to anyone. Then the daughter said, "Also, I beg you to forgive every sin that I might have committed against you."

She replied, "God will forgive you, since I forgive you what I'm able to forgive." The daughter couldn't hold back any longer, since it seemed she had waited a thousand years to give her mother this joy, and in one stroke Montanina stood up weeping and flung her arms around her mother's neck, hugging her tenderly and saying, "My sweet mother, I am your daughter Montanina, and you are my dear mother."

When the mother heard these words, she stood up almost mad with joy and put her hands on Montanina's shoulders and held her face a short distance from hers. She stared at her steadily. The surprise was so great that she almost fainted, and she would have fallen to the floor if her daughter had not held her up and set her to rest upon the bed. She quickly recovered, and the daughter embraced and kissed her. Hugging her daughter tightly, the mother said, "How can this be? I saw you and believed you were dead. Now you're alive in my arms and it's been twenty-five months and four days since I believed that you were dead. I have to be sure about this." Remembering a birthmark that her daughter had on the left side of her back, she unfastened her dress and realized that she truly was her daughter. Now you have to appreciate the joy that she felt without making me describe it. After many affectionate embraces, they sat down together again, since the mother wanted to know how all this was possible and how it could happen. The mother promised to forgive her daughter everything, and so Montanina described everything point by point.

When she described how Vannino became involved because of his love, she claimed that he was involved against his will, and she said that she was forced to go along with the situation in order to save her own honor. Montanina knew how to describe all this in such a way that her loving mother believed everything, just as she did when she told her how she had been transformed from a native of Perugia into a Milanese lady. In the end, the mother and daughter saw everything eye to eye, and together, they and Vannino decided, very discreetly, that the mother would always remain with them in their house. To ensure that Montanina would not be recognized as her daughter, they made these arrangements.

Montanina's mother had problems with her brother-in-law, who was given to quarreling and bickering. She went on complaining about her brother-in-law throughout the city, saying that he had robbed her and that she could not find justice in Perugia. Because she had been abandoned by her relatives, she said that she would entrust herself to anyone who would defend her and who would not be bothered by her relatives. She often went shouting throughout the city, complaining of the wrong that her brother-in-law had done to her so that throughout all of Perugia she was known for being a desperate woman who had been wronged and who would devote herself to whomever would help her.

She and Vannino arranged that one day in the piazza Vannino would be among a group of citizens when she arrived and, as she usually did, started complaining. She turned toward Vannino and said, "Vannino, I implore you, since I have neither friend nor relative who will help me, I beg you, take pity on me for the love of my blessed child, Montanina, whom you so honestly loved." Then she told him what she needed so everyone there felt compassion for her and she said, "Vannino, if you defend me from that traitorous brother-in-law of mine I will put my faith in you and give you title to everything that I have in the world, and I will stay with you always and regard you as a son. I beg you for the love of God and of that woman whom you loved so much."

Vannino, wise as he was, gestured to her to speak more slowly, and she, as arranged, said very outspokenly, "I want to be heard. I find it very important that these valiant citizens are here, because I want everyone in Perugia to know that I find in them neither justice nor good behavior, and so, in desperation I will give you all that I have in the world. Nothing will keep me tied to my kin if you'll defend me so that my brother-in-law can't harm me." Then she threw herself at the feet of those citizens, imploring them and speaking her mind, saying, "Because I am a widow and don't have a person who will help me I want to have a notary make out a deed for all my possessions to go to you, Vannino, if you promise to help me in the presence of those people who govern Perugia with so little ability." And although the citizens consoled her with words, she wouldn't stop moaning or speaking about giving the deed to Vannino if he would accept it.

Everyone encouraged Vannino to accept her offer, and a relative of Vannino said, "My good lady, if you want to carry out what you've said, I see a notary there whom I'll hire into your service, if you wish, and I will bring him here or wherever you like." She quickly replied that this was indeed what she wanted.

Vannino, like a wise man, wanted to make it all seem legitimate and said, "Don't be hasty, my lady. Without your deed, I would be pleased to help you as if you were my own dear mother, considering who your daughter was, so that you won't be harmed."

She beckoned to the man who offered to go for the notary. He was quick and brought the notary there. Vannino pretended to refuse and not to want the deed but, when the notary came, he relented, and as circumstances and she demanded, he was forced to accept her terms. The notary drew up the document. Under Vannino's wise authority she put the title of right to all of her endowments and to everything that she owned, on the sole condition that he would keep her in his home, support her, and look after her honorably for the rest of her life. After all, it was only proper that he would help her so that she wouldn't be robbed by her brother-in-law.

Vannino, who seemed to be forced by that woman's prayers and by the advice of those around him, was satisfied and led her to his house. She sent for what she had in her house and entrusted herself to him to take care of her as long as she lived, and Vannino did not regard her as any less than his own mother. So there she remained very happy with him throughout her life, and there was never anyone who suspected that she was his mother-in-law. Vannino had good reason to help her, and he defended her and acquired her rights, and they always lived together in good peace. Pellegrina, as a Lombard and as Vannino's wife, lived her life in happiness and joy. The jealous Andreoccio lamented Montanina's death and was scorned and derided, while Vannino was satisfied with what he had always wanted. And the wise Montanina preserved her honor and was always known as Pellegrina of Milan. With this deception, her wish came true.

SIR GIOVANNI DA PRATO & BALDINA

Gentile Sermini

🦂

Sir Michele Raffacanti, Podesta of Prato, was an extremely rich young man because his father always lent money at usurious rates. Because he was so pompous, he led a life that was more ostentatious than honorable. He lived with his wife, Mona Chiara, and his lovely fifteen-year-old daughter by his first wife, Baldina, who was, therefore, Mona Chiara's step-daughter. Sir Michele wanted to act as if he led the life of a lord, so he lived in a rented house instead of a courtly palace to limit his expenses. As a result, his wife slept with his daughter, while he and his servant, a handsome youth, slept in the corner of another room. Mona Chiara was unhappy with this arrangement, and she was a sensible and shrewd woman. Since there was already a young squire living in the house who was a well-groomed, handsome youth named Sir Ugolino, she said to him one morning, "Squire, you're a fine writer. I know how to read but not how to write: I've decide that you'll teach me how to write."

He replied, "My lady, I'd be pleased."

Then she said to him, "Since the master lies down and goes to bed every afternoon at three o'clock you'll have an hour or more to teach me without anyone knowing anything about it, and there's no better place than in your room."

Sir Ugolino responded, "My lady, I'm at your service." So they arranged to begin that afternoon.

When it was time for the Podesta to go to bed, Mona Chiara arrived at the squire's room, and so they wouldn't be interrupted, she locked the door to the room from inside. They sat together with their backs toward the fire and with every writing instrument on the table before them. Sir Ugolino began by taking a pen in his hand and was ready to write down some verse. She took a pen and with its point began to make use of the ink. She progressed from good to better, since she was by nature inclined to writing and because she worked hard at it. In a very short time she was able to write quite adequately. She took such delight in writing that she spent many afternoons with the squire, eager to learn all that she could from him. Because she felt at ease with him, very confident in his ability, she knew that he had no less regard for her than her very own husband, Sir Michele had. Therefore, she spent many more afternoons in bed with him, and her fantasies dwelt so much on writing that all the time that she lay with him she either wrote or she spoke about writing, and, if she slept, she always dreamt of writing.

After about two months, Sir Ugolino said to Mona Chiara, "I want to teach Baldina too, so that when you return to Florence both of you will be good writers." She said that she didn't want Baldina to learn, but he persisted and said to her, "If you don't let me teach her, don't count on learning any more from me." Finally she had to go along with this because she didn't want to forget what she had learned. And so, since she was pressured into it, she agreed to allow him to teach Baldina one night and her the next night. Mona Chiara and Baldina continued their instruction until there was not a woman in the country who wrote better than they did, so there wouldn't be one person who wouldn't be amazed if they only once saw them guide a pen in such sweet and skillful ways and with such fine strokes, following all the proper rules of writing. Baldina continued to write very well and her first ostrich quill was frequently sharpened, but little by little it began to fail and had to be replaced with a goose quill. Although the inkwell was always ready, the point of the pen couldn't bear so much writing. It needed temperance and discretion in its use.

Meanwhile Sir Ugolino had a friend, a clever notary from Prato, whose name was Sir Giovanni Da Prato. He was an expert in the scrivener's art of the notary. He was in love with Baldina and revealed his heart when he confided in Sir Ugolino, knowing him well enough to ask him urgently for any help he could offer. Sir Ugolino promised to arrange matters so that one night Sir Giovanni would find himself in a room alone with Baldina. He arranged it so that one Thursday night, while the Podesta was sleeping, Sir Giovanni found himself in Sir Ugolino's bedroom at dinner with him and Baldina. The three of them dined merrily together, and after dinner, since the night was still young, they continued their party. There was a book of Dante on the table, which delighted Sir Giovanni, and he began to read from it. The squire said, "I have to go meet someone. Wait here, and if I'm delayed too long, just sleep here." Then he left.

Inside the locked room Sir Giovanni continued to read with Baldina by his side. And he went on and on, and after he had already read and expounded on three chapters, he began reading the fourth. It was almost as if he didn't notice Baldina, and it became clear that he had a greater appetite for Dante than for her. She became indignant and being very crafty and clever she said to herself, "Perhaps this man expects me to encourage him. But it seems to me that he has come here to hold a class on Dante. If that's true, then he can stay here with Dante." And she quickly got up to leave.

As she opened the door, Sir Giovanni heard her and asked, "Where are you going, my lovely lady?"

She answered, "I'll return soon."

He believed her and she quickly slipped into Mona Chiara's bedroom, locking the door behind her. She got into bed and stayed there all night.

While waiting for Baldina, Sir Giovanni read the fourth chapter at his leisure, since he had to wait anyway. Finally, when Baldina didn't return, he realized that he had been deceived and he left feeling very sad.

🦎

When I arrived back at Prato the next morning, Sir Giovanni began to tell me about his escapade, and he complained about it in a friendly way, since we had been business acquaintances and friends for a long time, having attended the university together in our city. When he described his bad fortune, he moaned and groaned, complaining over and over, "O Fortune, what have I done to you that you are so against me?" He continued to lament his bad fortune rather than acknowledge that he was the cause of it. I looked him in the eye and took great pleasure in his story – reexamining everything again – and I laughed so hard that I couldn't even answer him.

BINDACCINO DA FIESOLE

Gentile Sermini

🦂

Among the many people at the baths at Petriuolo there was a youth from Fiesole named Bindaccino who was there for about a year because of a certain malady. He was a petulant, fast-talking person and also a scrounger. He would always carry a little sparrow-hawk on his fist, more for show than for hunting, and he learned about the opportunities and customs of the bath, where it's very expensive to live, so that he figured out how to support himself at other people's expense. He knew how to spend most of the day with other people, from morning to night, dining and eating without ever spending any of his own money, excusing himself from day to day by saying that he expected money from home at any time, and promising to repay his companions when it arrived. And when a new person would arrive at the bath who seemed able to spend money, he would quickly introduce himself, saying "Welcome. Do you need anything?" He would then busy himself with arrangements for the newcomer, procuring a room for him and space for his horses, recommending him to the innkeeper, saying "This man is an upstanding gentleman, make sure you treat him well." Then he would say to the guest, "Is there anything in particular that you'd prefer to dine on this evening? Please tell me what you would relish most and leave it to me to arrange." With these attentions and flattering words he welcomed the new guest, always staying close by until he was lodged, helping to arrange his things and acting so solicitous that it was necessary for him to stay with this friend for dinner. He did this to everyone. If he wasn't invited to go carousing, he invited himself.

As soon as the guests were wise to his ways, they gave him crumbs, but others, who were just newly arrived, didn't understand this.

At one point four honorable young men arrived from Siena. Bindaccino quickly gravitated to them, holding their stirrups when they dismounted, proffering himself and assisting them in whatever they needed. He tried to please these men so much that they considered him an honest young man, nobly educated and courteous and, since they felt themselves obligated to him, they invited him to stay for dinner. He accepted, saying he was a little short of cash, but adding that he expected money to arrive from home any day now.

Those men said, "Don't worry about anything. Come join us both morning and night."

Then Bindaccino said, "To tell you the truth I feel ashamed, but because you're such decent young men I whole-heartedly accept your invitation. I wouldn't dare say yes to this rabble I find myself with, but I'd be de-lighted to go along with you." They saw his polite appearance, his sparrow-hawk, and his fine dress, with only a small patch on his sleeve. They assumed that he was who he said he was, but after a few days they quickly realized what kind of person he was. Since it seemed that they were being duped, they decided to play a trick on him. Weaving together a good plot, they praised his knowledge and skill, which included knowing how to cook every kind of dish. So one day, since they had only a little money left, they brought two little stomachs of lamb to him. He said, "I want to cook them with my own hands because you'll never taste a better dish." So they let him do as he wished, and he delicately cooked the innards.

Not only the proprietor, but the entire household disliked Bindaccino, especially the cook, Venturello, who was a very astute person. He had a pair of foul drawers that were the receptacle for chewed food in the common room, since they were often used to wipe many mouths whenever the need arose. Then, because they were so foul, they were carelessly tossed at the back of the kitchen where all the unwashed pots and pans and other slop were thrown. They were soaked in this mixture so that the two well-cooked stomachs were not yet as tender as those soaked drawers that were left in that odiferous and mellow mire. Venturello and the proprietors agreed that they would give Bindaccino those drawers to eat in exchange for the tripe.

When everything was arranged the proprietors dined well on their good food early in the day, and then the proprietor of the bath summoned Bindaccino and said to him, "I see you're fit and able. The truth is that I want to make a fine and respectable dinner for all the patrons of the bath, and I'd be honored if you'd be the director."

Bindaccino said to him, "Don't worry. Leave it to me to prepare a meal of chicken, pigeons, goats, wine, and whatever else you need."

The owner thanked him, and held him to his word, nodding as he left. The four youths had already dined and were playing chess at the table. Thanks to the owner, Bindaccino was, of course, running around the house. He discovered that the youths had dined, and that the servants were now at the table. He said to them, falling into mockery himself, "Were those stomachs good?"

The servants responded that yes, they were, and that they had put his portion aside. But Venturello had arranged everything ahead of time and had put those delicate drawers on the fire in a little pot. He filled the pot with the broth from the stomachs, mixed the stomachs about with the drawers, and plotted with the servants. A certain Arrigo Tedesco, who had conspired with the proprietors when it was decided that the cook would see to it that Bindaccino would eat this meal, sprang into action and arranged a medley of so many spices and so much grated cheese with that broth that, at first, Bindaccino would not detect any hint of the drawers. He put the drawers and half of the little stomachs in a wooden bowl while Bindaccino sat down at the table with a good appetite. Arrigo cut and mixed the stomach and drawers in front of him. Bindaccino ate voraciously and his great appetite led him to eat at times a morsel of stomach and at other times a morsel of drawers. The spices prevented him from discerning the flavor of the stewed drawers. And he didn't notice the morsels of drawers he was eating, since he couldn't mince them with his teeth, and so he gulped them down without chewing, though at times he could taste something bad. Since Bindaccino himself had cooked the stomachs, he forced himself as well as he could to pretend that they seemed fine to him, but wearily, time and again, he swallowed great wads of the drawers. Then he put a great big morsel of drawers in his mouth, and trying to cut it in two with his teeth, he couldn't because he had bitten into the laces. He fought with both of his hands to pull all the laces out of his mouth and seeing them he said, "What the devil is this?"

Venturello, who hadn't paid attention to anything else, went over to him, took him by the hand, and quickly turned with an agitated expression to that servant who made the stew, shouting, "Arrigo, what have you done? What pot did you use to make this stew?"

As was arranged, Arrigo said, "How do I know? I found two pots with stomachs. I put one on top of the other and put the stew and all the other things in a tower of pots. I put them in one wooden bowl and brought it to Bindaccino. Who knows? I did what my master said. What have you done that such a wriggling mass of worms have sprung from your mouth?"

Venturello said, "For pity's sake, Tedesco, sweet dreams, you're already drunk before you even wake up. The one pot had the stomachs that were set aside, but the other pot had a pair of foul drawers that I found in the filthy alley where we toss out everything from the kitchen. Before that they were used by many mouths for other purposes. But they were so filthy, I put them in an ash pan over the fire to clean them. Now you've given them to someone to eat and have made such a fragrant broth that a mass of worms sprouts from it. Even pigs would be disgusted by it, never mind people! And to prove it, here are the ties of the drawers." He showed them to Bindaccino and to everyone else in the party.

Everyone had a great laugh, except Bindaccino. Bindaccino, like the others, forced himself to laugh, but he couldn't really because he felt sick to his stomach. Thanks to his stomach and his shame, he couldn't eat another bite, and all that day he was sad and sick from that meal.

Now that evening, the whole party went to the bath where they amused and enjoyed themselves as they usually did. While the proprietor and his council were holding parliament in the bath, they were joined by Venturello. Arrigo, the servant, was called before the proprietor regarding a pair of drawers that he had made Bindaccino eat. Although he knew the whole story, the proprietor pretended that this was all news to him, and he made Venturello tell the whole story out loud, from the beginning, so that everyone in the bath would hear him. The proprietor made Arrigo come over to him and said, "I want to hear the other side." When he asked Arrigo. how this had happened, Arrigo said, "The worms spouted on the fire. I found two pots on the fire. I thought they both contained stomachs. I mixed one with the other and put them in a bowl, adding grated cheese and spices to make a good broth, and I brought the whole stew to Bindaccino. Whoever put the drawers in the stew brought the devil. I did what my master commanded."

Venturello had brought the ties and some morsels from the cut-up drawers with him and showed them to the proprietor and to the whole company. The proprietor laughed and called Bindaccino saying, "Is what Venturello says true?"

He forced himself to say, "It was that blockhead Arrigo. He was drunk."

Arrigo said, "Me, blockhead? You lie through your teeth. You're the dunce who eats drawers, not me."

Two more came in and stood in front of the proprietor and said that they had heard that Bindaccino really liked drawers but they didn't believe it. Now they saw that it was true. He had eaten the two pairs of drawers that they had lost, and they asked the proprietor to make amends. Then a shout went round the baths to Bindaccino saying, "Bindaccino eats drawers!" As they kept chanting this they took Bindaccino and led him in front of the proprietor, where they quickly tied his hands behind his back and put the drawers on his head. Then he was put on display and buffeted all around the bath. They said, "Quit eating drawers."

After that evening, the bath remained a merry place for many days, but during that night, the reviled Bindaccino raised camp without a trumpet call, and he never returned to the bath. Afterward, he was always known in Fiesole as Bindaccino of the Drawers, and at the bath whoever loses or mislays their drawers always says, "I've lent them to Bindaccino."

DOLCIBENE

Giovanni Gherardi da Prato

Most delightful company, it's well known to everyone,
high and low, who considers all the aspects of our city,
that it has had the greatest abundance of unusual wits. At
present I'll be silent about all except one, commemorat-
ing him and telling a story about him and his famous art,
because his profession is slandered by many who prefer to
revile it rather than call it an art. It's the fault of the sad
and indecent craftsmen who've fallen into ruin and
gluttons who practice the art, not with the decent gaiety
and mirth that the art requires, but rather as rascals, sting-
ing, insulting, and abusing both verbally and physically in
every unpleasant way and indecent manner. These should
be drowned and beaten, rather than heard or welcomed.
Those craftsmen might truthfully be called men of the
court, but commonly and more properly, they're called
fools.

There was a citizen from here, virtuous and cunning
who, even as a boy, took delight in the courts. His name
was Sir Dolcibene, and he was a knight of no small
reputation. As we'll see, he became very sorry and infa-
mous for getting involved in a very big mix-up, but
Charles of Luxembourg, King of the Romans, decorated

him with military honors and gave him privileges and made him King of all the Fools.

Dolcibene was handsome and had a robust and vigorous body. He was a proper musician and an excellent player of the hurdy-gurdy, the lute, and other instruments. Sir Bernabò and Sir Galeazzo Visconti of Milan and their honorable and magnificent court learned of the fame and felicity of Dolcibene, and he decided to go to make his living there, and so he did. He was welcomed and became known for his talents in making rhythmic ditties with pleasant words and singing them with very sweet song. For his skill he received many gifts from many gentlemen and lords who then found themselves at this court. For some time Sir Dolcibene lived happily and pleasantly with profit and amusement until that same year a similar man of the court arrived in Milan.

He was Sir Mellon dalla Pontenara, knighted by Sir Ubertino of Carrara, Lord of Padua. He was a handsome man with a proud face and powerful physique, and he became acquainted with Sir Dolcibene. But the courtiers provoked them so that each one began to torment and slander the other until finally Sir Mellon said that Sir Dolcibene had the face of a poltroon, and that it would be best if he went back to Florence to eat rotten salad, and didn't speak to esteemed knights.

Sir Dolcibene was very proud and, when he was presented the opportunity, he replied, "Sir Mellon, you speak licentiously and you're a blockhead, so I promise you and swear, in case you have any doubt, that because you've eaten so many fish in Pontenara your head is filled with slime, so that you're a great beast and a pathetic, evil man. And I'll be ready at any time to prove this to you with a weapon in my hand."

Sir Mellon, who had a similar opinion of Dolcibene, was incited and provoked by many gentlemen of the court until he decided to tell them that he was ready to prove to them that his opponent not only lied through his teeth, but that he spoke nonsense and embodied every wickedness and evil. Sir Mellon said this in front of the two lords and the many knights and squires.

The lords, who saw these madmen behaving like beasts, were very amused and only half-heartedly discouraged their lunacy. But then each of the fools boasted that he was the handsomest and bravest. So Sir Bernabò said, "Sir Dolcibene, since you want to preserve your honor, which is something I commend in you, I'll put you on the field of battle, and you'll bear no expense for it at all."

When he heard this, Sir Galeazzo said the same thing to Sir Mellon. So, they began to provoke one another ver- bally even more, each one asking his respective lord to set the field and day of battle. They reserved the field on the piazza. On Saint George's day they decided that the bat- tle would take place on Saint Michael's day, the eighth day of May. That left eighteen days – plenty of time before the battle for each one to make his arrangements.

Each knight was outfitted and ready, but when they thought back on what had happened, each judged himself very unwise. Sir Dolcibene said to himself, "For God's sake, Dolcibene, what have you done? You mock and torment all the world with jokes and hoaxes and pranks, and now you give everyone who sees, knows, and hears about this a reason to mock you. You have put yourself in peril with your madness! You know that Sir Mellon is brave, strong, and spirited, just like you, and you also know that in spite of everything, he has no reason to fight with you, just as you have no reason to fight with him. And what could come of this? You'll kill each other, or you him, or he you. Who knows what will happen? Except something dangerous. And everyone will be laughing at you and mocking you and thinking that you're both two solemn blockheads. Everyone will be waiting for this battle with the greatest amusement. What, then, will you be called – unfortunate, naive or a little fool? Now you mock the world, but you see, because of your folly the world will mock you." And so, with these things on his mind Sir Dolcibene lamented his own lack of sense, and as the date approached, he lamented his error even more.

Sir Mellon had similar regrets. He felt he had set off on the worst possible path, but he didn't want to say anything that might increase the damage. He considered Sir Dolcibene mighty, spirited, and brave, and he waited for the morning of combat with the greatest fear, although each of them displayed great courage and gave the impression of looking forward to the coming battle.

At the appointed hour a great crowd filled the stands to see the most ferocious brawl. Sir Dolcibene was armed extremely well and accompanied by the knights and squires of Sir Bernabò whose camp he represented. He waited for Sir Mellon, begging God that if He would answer his prayer that Sir Mellon wouldn't come to the field of battle, he would visit the Holy Land.

While he was making these vows, Sir Mellon, extremely well armed, accompanied by the family of Sir Galeazzo, approached the field. And there the two knights who would guide the course of the duel performed certain ceremonies and made each of them swear that they would toss their gauntlets into the field, since that was the cus-tom, so that they could commence the duel. But Sir Dolcibene, quick-witted and sane, said, "Most esteemed knights, I want to say a few words before beginning the battle, because I haven't a single doubt that at least one of us, if not both together, shall die. To me it seems that for the good of our souls he ought to forgive me in the event that I die, and I ought to do likewise to him, kissing him on the lips."

The knights said that they could do as they pleased. Then Sir Dolcibene approached his adversary and lifted the visor of his helmet. Speaking softly so that he wouldn't be heard by anyone but his opponent, he said "It seems to me that we're two great fools and we've come here to kill ourselves to delight these people. I, for myself, regret all of this, and I don't want to put myself in this danger. I don't know what you think."

Sir Mellon responded instantly, "I think the same thing, and the same thought just occurred to me, but by now it's too late for us to mend our ways."

Sir Dolcibene said, "It's never too late, if you want to stop this."

He replied, "That's what I want, by God! For pity sake, go on, by God, that's what I want, and I offer you my complete trust."

"Now, in the name of God, do exactly as I do," Sir Dolcibene said.

He gladly replied, "Yes, certainly." And they quickly kissed each other on the lips as a sign of the faith each would keep with the other.

The spectators remained silent, waiting for the fierce duel. Sir Dolcibene tossed in the gauntlet of battle and brandished a lance in his hand from his side of the field. He touched the point to the ground and then lifted it in one shot and hurled it to the ground. Sir Mellon saw this and did the same thing. Then Sir Dolcibene took a hatchet, and a few times he pretended to assault Sir Mellon with it, and then he threw it away. Sir Mellon quickly did the same thing. Then he took his sword and made feints and bellicose blusterings, and he now pretended to jab and cut and he spent a good long time with Sir Mellon doing the same. Finally they threw the swords to the ground and took their daggers into their hands. Then each one attacked the other many times without ever touching his opponent. They amazed everyone. Then Sir Bernabò watched the duel and said, "You see how these two lunatics want to fight hand to hand and to the finish."

For a long time they deceived the onlookers, finally throwing away the daggers as they had done with the other weapons. Once they did this, each one moved away, returning to his own corner. Baring their hips, they stripped themselves and ran at each other with a tremendous force so that they collided together. This caused the greatest laughter in the world because, since both of them were quite large and fleshy, their buttocks made an explosive noise that in the collision sounded like a bomb.

The people, especially the knights, soon realized they were being deceived, and they said to them, "Since you've made fools of us, you'll certainly pay for it."

It's your fault," Sir Dolcibene said, "since this trade is our money, this is how we pay. If you wish, we're ready to make even greater payment to you, so that you'll be satisfied."

It seemed to Sir Bernabò and Sir Galeazzo that these two had perceived their peril very well, and the lords wanted to know in complete detail how the event unfolded and which one of them had first checked their madness. Sir Mellon told them everything, and they were astonished at the quick and pleasant solution of Sir Dolcibene, whom they congratulated.

So you see the very quick wisdom of the pleasant Sir Dolcibene, and how he was able to parry danger with such charm and cunning that one can't begin to imagine, much less hope, to do the same thing in a similar circumstance.

BERTO & MORE

Giovanni Gherardi da Prato

🦌

*Unhappy with their lives, two companions, Berto and More complain about their neighbors and discuss leaving Florence...*More concludes, "and no one would have believed him if he weren't one of the Flagellants. We're led by mere hypocrites, and God knows who they are. Just yesterday morning an oil merchant who sold fritters of millet was all of a sudden appointed the official in charge of food provisions and captain of the kitchen detail of Santo Michele Lapo of the Cross. Now, think of how we live. Berto, let's go at once to Hungary and stay with the King and leave behind these disgraceful people here."

Berto listened to More and learned from him that Hungary was a wealthy country. Because he hadn't lived in Florence for very long, he decided to do whatever More liked, though he found it difficult to lose sight of Giotto's campanile. He said, "More, since you've decided to go and stay with your nephew Giovanni in Hungary, I'd be pleased to go with you. But I'd still like to discuss with you a little about how people live there. At the moment, let's not discuss it any further, but after we dine we'll talk about it at length, since we'll be in better spirits, and we'll understand it more completely."

"Come on now," said More. "I'd be happy to take your advice."

So, they went to Mombellozza's inn outside the city walls near the Porta al Prato. There they ordered sprouts and onion stew after first eating a piece of herb pie with horehound. They dined with great pleasure, drinking plenty of good wine, and after they finished, they sat in a sunny place for a little while, and there they began again to discuss the wisdom of going to Hungary. They discussed it so carefully that great masters would have been happy with their opinions.

Berto became a little tipsy from the wine, and he began to boast saying, "Alas, More, let's go as quickly as we can, because I've made a vow to God that if we arrive there safe and sound, you'll see me become a great master in a short time. I'll let my beard grow, and I'll always carry a bow with me. Let's go at once!"

More replied, "I like what you're saying. It would be best for us to go to Borgo San Lorenzo and speak with Cavallina. He'll find a way for us to have two horses, the best that he can find, to take us as far as Bologna."

Berto quickly replied, "Now, when do we want to go? Wouldn't it be better to get them from Agnolo, since he always has the best? Let's go to him."

"Oh, simpleton," More said. "You don't understand these things! I want you to know that, beside being a dealer, Cavallina is the best rider in all Florence. You'd rather go to Agnolo who I think is a liar. For heaven's sake, leave it to More Feci to arrange things and we'll be off on the day after Candlemass, that's Tuesday!"

Berto answered, "Come on now, we'll do whatever you want! I think you're a better judge of these things than I am."

They drank a bit more after their discussion and then left Mombellozza. They went to the Borgo and hired two horses from Cavallina for their day of departure. Each one put his affairs in order as best he could or knew how. Each one carried only a game-bag with his night-cap inside and what little money he had, climbed on his horse, and set off on the road toward Bologna. When they finally arrived, Berto and More shared a room with a coachman they met along the way, and they all complained about how tired they were. In the end, the coachman decided to travel to Hungary with them. They went to sleep and rested well the whole night.

In the morning they settled their account with the innkeeper and set off on the road again. At last they reached Venice where they boarded a ship that landed at Zara. After they very happily arrived at Zara they hurried on the road to Buda. When they reached Buda, they were warmly welcomed by Giovanni, More's nephew. While discussing with him and some other Florentines who were there all the new things that they had seen, Berto said, "What good does it do to describe them? I would never have believed it if I hadn't seen it for myself. It was the most amazing thing I've ever seen. It leaves me speechless."

The Florentines said, "For pity sake, Berto, tell us. Here everything's possible."

Berto strained to describe what he had seen and replied, "I'll tell you because you ask. Since we arrived here from across the sea we've found little children of five and six

years of age who speak Hungarian, and to those who understand that language their speech is a joy, while our
Florentine children of that age hardly know how to speak
it at all. And they say that there are some children who
have a better memory than I, myself, would ever believe
possible to find, except among the elderly. To me, all of
this seems like the Epiphany."

Not waiting for Berto to say anything else, More
quickly added, "He's telling the truth. I, for one, would
never have believed it. I thought that my cousin, as
chatty as she is, had a good memory. But she doesn't
know how to speak anything but Florentine, and she
doesn't know any Hungarian."

Giovanni, listening to them, was astonished by their ig-
norance and stupidity, and he stared at them fixedly
without saying anything. Berto thought that he didn't
believe them, and he said, "Upon the body of God it's
true, Giovanni! Haven't you heard it?"

The Florentines who were there began to laugh but
they didn't want to upset such good men so soon after
their arrival. After they delighted the company with their
chatter, it came time to rest, and they went off to sleep.

When the morning came and More said to his relative,
"Giovanni, we'd like to visit the King. Please arrange it
so we can see him. Where is he now?"

Giovanni quickly said, "You can't see him right now
because he's on Margaret Island, and not in Buda."

"Where's this island?" Berto asked. "Are you teasing
me? For pity's sake, don't joke about things that are so
important. I remind you that I've come here to see him!
Don't you know that in Florence we described this visit a
thousand times? For pity's sake, now that we're here,

how could we return to Florence and say that we didn't see the King? We'd be considered fine idiots by the whole neighborhood."

They weren't able to persuade Giovanni to arrange an audience with the King, so Berto, More, and the coachman went to wander through the city of Buda down to the banks of the Danube. There, in the middle of the river, they spotted Margaret Island and realized that it must be the island that Giovanni mentioned, so they crossed over to it. Once on the island, they met a gentleman who spoke their language. When he asked them why they came to visit Hungary, they told him that they had come to see the King. But they didn't realize that they were in the presence of the King himself.

"I, for myself, still want to see him," said More. "Don't you think that he's a great King? I hear that he keeps seventy thousand horses in his fields. Is this true or no, my good man?"

The King replied, "He certainly keeps them in his realm."

And so, they discussed many, many things, and the King stayed with them, taking great pleasure in their company. Meanwhile, five hours passed, and all the barons had dined and returned to Margaret Island from Buda.

The King and his companions walked as far as the doors of the royal garden and found them locked. They knocked at the door and two pages came to a small window in the door and said that they've been commanded not to open it. The archbishop asked who was with the King, and the pages told him that they believed the men were Latins. The archbishop hesitated but realized that the doors would not open themselves so he told the boys to open the doors, at least to see who was with the King. They opened the doors, thrust their heads outside and saw the King standing with these men, and they came out even farther.

The coachman, who saw the archbishop, said, "Berto, by God's body, look at that glutton who has just turned his back," and he began to laugh loudly. Berto saw him and started laughing too.

The King saw the barons inside the garden, and a bad mood came over him because he thought he would lose the pleasure of the company of these men. While the archbishop moved closer, More said, "Who are these people? Now we can see how silly it is to come to Buda. Why are they coming to you? Do they want to hear stories of the King too?"

While he was speaking, the archbishop along with the other barons paid their proper respects to the King, kneeling and greeting him. The King answered their greetings by saying, "You've taken away the greatest joy that I've ever had, speaking with these Florentine friends of mine. Since you left I've been here with them like good friends."

Seeing how these men deferred to their companion, More and his friends were astonished, and although they were slouching before, they now stood straight up on their feet. They began to feel ashamed, since they realized that this man had to be the King, and it seemed to them that they had behaved shamefully. Almost bewildered, they didn't know what to say, and the King said to them, "Good fellows, go with this page to eat something, and once you've dined I'll see you. Now go quickly." The

King called the page and told him that he should take them to Luca of Florence who should pay them homage.

Stunned, those men went with the page, asking him if that man was the King. The page, who didn't understand them, said to them in Hungarian, "Come on now, come come!"

They didn't understand the page and thought that he was cursing at them, and in great dread they reached Luca. This man had watched them for a good part of their time there, and he said, "Oh you crazy fools, aren't you ashamed for what you've done, you ill-bred, fat brutes? Who did you think he might have been? Who did you think you were with, when you spoke with the King while you went toddling along? I might be mad but I think I might do some good if I took a stick and beat you like two asses. Curses on you! Because of you every Florentine will feel shame. Who the devil did you think he was? For pity's sake, tell me!"

More replied, "You see, Luca, we would have never believed that he was the King because he didn't wear a crown on his head. We thought he was a priest."

When he heard this simpleton, Luca couldn't restrain himself, but he laughed a little and then he said, "For pity's sake, go back to Florence as quickly as you can, and don't go strolling around!"

Then he brought them inside and gave them something to eat, and once they had eaten, they decided to return quickly to Buda. But Luca wanted them to return to the King, since this was what the King wanted, and he thought it best to teach them the respects they should pay to him, instructing them so they wouldn't forget.

They returned to the King, and when he saw them arrive, he stepped toward them saying, "Welcome, my Florentines!"

They stooped to the ground with great shame and More started to say, "Sir, forgive us because, in good faith, we didn't know that you were the King since, if we had known, we would never have behaved in such a familiar way with you."

The King answered, "I wanted you to behave just as you did."

Berto added, "Sir, God wouldn't like it, nor want it. We want you as our King and superior, but then we thought that you were a priest."

The King laughed and said to them, "Don't leave. Stay with me."

"Now what would my nephew Giovanni say if I didn't return to his house this evening? He would fret and fume. But we will return another time and stay all day with you. Please allow us to go this time."

The King agreed, provided that they would do precisely as they promised and return another time. So they took their leave of the King and returned to Buda.

Their story spread quickly throughout Buda, and they were much reproved for their ways. But they had no other excuse but to say, "Good, fine, why doesn't he wear a crown on his head so he can be recognized?"

You see how simple these pin-heads were. So, it seems to me that the mercy of such a great prince who forgave these three foolish, inexperienced, and thick-headed little companions is worthy of no little praise.

GIACOPPO

Lorenzo de' Medici

As many of you must know, there's always been an abundance of simpletons and a good number of block-heads in Siena. I don't know why the atmosphere there naturally produces such a breed of men, but perhaps they all come from the same tree that grew from such a bad seed that it's natural to expect that the fruit would have to be as bad as the original seed. They say that a good boy takes after his father, and perhaps that's why these sons – who don't want to shame their fathers or appear to be bastards – behave just as badly as their fathers.

Not many years ago in Siena there lived a citizen named Giacoppo Belanti. He was about forty years old and rather wealthy but also a bit stupid. Among his ventures, or should I say misadventures, was that he had married a very beautiful woman. In fact, beauty seems to be quite a natural thing among the women of Siena, just as it seems quite natural for the men to be foolish and conceited. His wife was about twenty-five years old and, like other beautiful women, she was admired by a hand-some young man. This gentle lady's name was Cassandra, and her young man was called Francesco. He was a citizen of Florence.

This young man had lived in Siena for a long time as a student and had always been in love with Cassandra. It's reasonable to expect that she was as fond of him as he was of her, especially when you consider that Francesco was a handsome youth, and she was already old enough to tell the difference between good and bad, and knew, by then, as much as a woman could know. She was truly at the age when a woman is a good lover, because when a woman is younger she is more likely to feel shame or regret, and after a certain age, she either thinks too much or becomes too cold to suit the needs of her lover.

Francesco had been pursuing her for quite some time, but was not yet successful in luring her into his trap. Now he was able to think of nothing else, day or night, except how to find a way to gain his greatest desire. And what fired his passion even more was that both parties were very willing, but only lacked the ways and means. Although Cassandra continued to love him, her love was chilled to some extent by her fear for her honor and of Giacoppo's jealousy. He treated her just as other husbands treat their beautiful wives, but since Cassandra was more beautiful than other women, she was less willing to tolerate her husband – a man already old and neither very handsome nor very stalwart in battle. Besides, she knew her husband was half an idiot.

All this gave Cassandra grounds to search for new options, and these reasons were enough to light a fire where there were never any coals. And anyway, this is a very natural thing to do: when you have the option to choose between the good and the bad, it's best to seize the good right away. On the contrary, she'd be crazy and fit to be tied if she did the opposite. It really seems to me that a woman has the great misfortune and a man the great advantage because a man, as small and unhappy as he might be, can choose a particular woman for his wife while a woman, not knowing why or how, always remains at the mercy of another's decision. A woman has to take what she's given and accept it so she doesn't end up with worse, and she has to be satisfied with things that are the cause of a thousand deaths every day. It's no surprise that every day one discovers that mistakes have been made. Things should be judged with greater care than we use now, and we should allow them to deduct nineteen coins out of twenty for these very reasons.

To return to our story, Cassandra and Francesco lacked nothing but the opportunity to make each other happy. Their greatest regret was that such a dolt was standing in their way. Giacoppo had managed with solicitude rather than intelligence to take away the lovers' ways and means.

Francesco thought the situation over, and over again, and relying on Giacoppo's simplicity and he came up with a plan that I'll describe to you. First, he pretended that he had totally abandoned his love for Cassandra. He kept this up for quite some time so that Giacoppo was almost sure that this was true. Then one day Francesco pretended that he had received a letter from relatives in Florence telling him that they had found a wife for him. This news soon traveled quickly among his friends and companions in Siena, because he was loved and known by so many people there. It wasn't long before the news reached Giacoppo's ears who, when he heard it, became happier than he had been for a long, long time since it seemed to him that now he could be sure of keeping his wife. Giacoppo believed that Francesco would have to leave Siena and forget about all his affairs there, just like anyone else who marries a wife.

Once Giacoppo was no longer suspicious, Francesco began to say that he didn't want to leave Siena at all because having studied so hard and endured so much he didn't want to abandon his work just when he was about to receive his doctorate. However, he had decided to bring his wife to Siena and provide for her there as best he could. After he made this clear to everyone, he rented a different house, because there wasn't enough room for him and his new wife in his first house. The new house was not far from where Giacoppo lived, and Giacoppo would often have to pass by there. It was only a short time before Francesco said he had to go to Florence to be married and to bring his wife to Siena, and so off he went to Florence to find a "woman of merit" among those who honestly, but publicly, practice their art. She was called Meina and had quite a pretty face and good appearance. She lived in the vicinity of Borgo Stella. He agreed to give her a lot of money if she would go away with him for a while. She was extremely willing and agreed to accompany him and meet with his honorable companions in Siena, letting him say that she was his wife, Bartolomea. Since everyone believed it was true, she was much honored by the gentlewomen of Siena and was a guest in their homes many times.

She was as astute as she was bad, and she knew very well how to disguise under her beautiful and feminine dress her innumerable blemishes. She pretended to have great honesty and to disdain dishonesty. She was well trained by Francesco in everything that she had to do. She sometimes sat at the window overlooking the street that Giacoppo frequently had to pass through, because it was on the way to his shop. After finding her at the balcony so often, he came upon his misfortune. She gave him a come-hither glance, and he cheerfully responded, although there had been many other times when he had wanted the fig blossom. Now he began to say to himself: "This is truly a fine thing. Francesco was in love with my wife, and it wasn't that long ago when he had to put on a good face, being young and handsome as he was. Now as old as I am, and in such a short time, I've already found favor with his wife. It seems as though Francesco wanted it to happen, just like a dog of Mainardo, who attacked to bite, but was himself the first morsel.

Stirred up as much by arrogance as by love, he found the route even more amenable, and Giacoppo began to increase his trips until one day he found himself, the one of advanced age, in a circle of youths and he was saying, "What has happened really is the result of an art that comes with age. You have all the time of your lives to cherish, but you won't conclude anything. As old as I am now, in a little while something great will happen to me, and I say no more." With all of his boasting however, he still didn't know how he would find the way or means to make his "confession."

That is, until one day. Since she hadn't heard from him, Bartolomea had to discreetly make the first move. She sent her maid to deliver a letter to him in which she wrote that she was dying for him and, for God's sake, could he help her, since she had no doubt that she was getting worse. With this news Giacoppo could not contain his happiness and he made a reply as stupid as he

was. Before long she showed him how difficult it was to
be a lover.

She gave him the chance for one night, saying that
Francesco had gone away to stay with one of his Sienese
companions. When evening finally came, which
Giacoppo felt he had waited for a thousand years, she
motioned for him to come into the house. Bartolomea
carried it all off like someone burning with great love. She
led him into the bedroom and put him under the sheets,
telling him that he had to stay there until she sent her
maid to bed, because she wanted things to go secretly. He
did as he was told and stayed there for about two and a
half hours. When Bartolomea returned she showed him
how sorry she was for his discomfort and said that he
would have to be patient. While they were together she
scratched his face, pulled open his eye, and bit his flesh –
leaving marks of affection, she said. He believed, of
course, that they were acting just like lovers, and he was
not only quiet and patient, but it seemed to him that he
could touch heaven with his finger.

In the end, although they had cherished one another for
so long and had endured a great deal of fatigue, even
though he was an old man, he managed to bring himself
where he wanted to go. She was amazed that at his age he
had succeeded so well, since she had made the poor little
man work himself to death in order to do what for him
seemed impossible. When he went home, he was more
dead than alive, all beaten and tottering, but feeling like
he had just come from paradise. He had another battle to
fight with his wife, and he wanted to vindicate himself by
doing in one night what, at another time, would not only

have been difficult, but impossible for him in an entire year.

Bartolomea, well taught by Francesco, didn't want the game to slip through her hands, so she continued to keep an eye on Giacoppo. Although he often came to see her, he didn't leave again for home without bites and scratches. They met many, many times, and kept it up for many, many months with both amorous words and deeds. He was so conceited that he would have gone on like this, continuing happily with both the new woman and the old without realizing that he was weaving a net in which he would soon be caught. But the good times continued for a while until Lent arrived. At that time Bartolomea begged Giacoppo that they should take a holiday from each other long enough to let the Holy Days pass. She told him that it was time to attend to the spirit, although it would be hard to be without him for a while.

These words inspired Giacoppo to go to confession and admit the guilt of his sins. He went to his old confessor, a Franciscan monk by the name of Brother Antonio Della Marca, with whom Francesco had already had discussions, since he knew that Giacoppo would confess everything to him. This man, although he was a brother who esteemed the seven works of mercy to help the afflicted, and although he wanted to prove the saying that Franciscans don't make traps or treachery, was easily persuaded to help Francesco. Giacoppo came to stand and confess as he generally did. When he came to the sin of lust, Giacoppo began to explain his affair with Francesco's wife, according to what he believed was going on. The brother stopped him saying, "Oh my, Giacoppo, how could you have had such a diabolical temptation to commit such an unpardonable sin? Without question it's not in my authority nor in the pope's nor even in Saint Peter's, if he returned to life, to be able to absolve you."

Giacoppo said, "Oh, I have heard it said that this isn't so great a sin that it can't possibly be absolved."

Brother Antonio responded, "True, but you need to do something that I know you would never do."

Giacoppo then said, "There is nothing I wouldn't do to save my soul, even confessing in the presence of my wife."

Brother Antonio said, "If you're sure of that, I'll tell you, but it seems certain to me that you'll promise me but you won't be terrified enough of me to keep your promise."

Giacoppo said, "You astonish me. I love my soul more than anything in this world."

Brother Antonio said, "All right, I'll tell you. Haven't you heard it said that the sin of infamy and of the things that man holds against reason can't be pardoned without restitution? This is true of your sin. Once you've stripped the honor from this man and his wife, you must give it back to them. And you can't give it back unless you allow this woman's husband or – if she has no husband – her closest male relative, to be with your wife just as many times – if you have a wife. If you don't have a wife then it should be with your nearest female relative, just as you were with his wife. Scripture says that when David committed the sin of adultery, he presented his wife to the person from whom he had taken the other woman, and so he was forgiven. So you see, this is what you have to do."

When Giacoppo heard the priest say this it seemed to him that he had done pretty badly, and he said to himself,

"I never thought I'd see the day when I'd become the dog of Mainardo." Then he turned to the brother and said, "Spiritual father, although it seems very difficult for me to understand this, I love my soul more than anything else in this world, and I mustn't be ashamed at all since David, who was a king, also did the same thing, and I'm just a citizen of Siena. Therefore I really want to save my soul rather than allow anything else to happen."

The brother listened to Giacoppo's pious words without saying anything else, but he embraced him and kissed his brow and face. He held him a little while and said, "My son in spirit, I see that the grace of God has en‐ lightened you, and I see that you're taking a path that will enable you to be a thousand times blessed. Today I see that nothing ever goes well without the Savior to thank for it. But I warn you, this sin of yours is so great that even with all this, one may still not be absolved without special penance. Therefore I have decided that you should go as far away as Rome to make amends for this sin and for your other sins. This is how one gains the glory of eternal life when he passes happily beyond this life. Therefore go blessed son, and carry out all that you have promised me." And he gave him his blessing.

Giacoppo, with his head full of thoughts, rose from the priest's feet and went home. Though he argued with himself, in the end his conscience won, and he decided to go and find Francesco and restore his lost honor to him. Then he realized another difficulty. He didn't know how he could tell this to Francesco without great risk to him‐ self. However, overcome by his conscience, he was determined to find a way to do it, since in the midst of the Holy Days, a person would be safer than at any other time. One day, therefore, he went to find Francesco and said, "Francesco, I've always loved you as a son, and at your age you could be. Sin has now led me to do something that I very much regret. I pray that you'll forgive me for it and that God will also forgive me. And before you say anything, promise me and swear not to take offense at me, but instead, for the martyrdom of our Lord, forgive the injury that I've given you."

Francesco said, "I've always held you in reverence like a father and when you die I promise, my father, to forgive you every offense that you have done to me, first for the love of God and then out of my love for you."

Giacoppo threw himself at his feet said, "I'll never tell you what I've done except on my knees."

With great effort Francesco made him stand up and began to listen to what he knew much better than Giacoppo himself. After Giacoppo, weeping, said what he had to say, Francesco pretended to be completely beside himself and said, "You had good reason to make me give you my word, because if I hadn't, before I left you I'd have done something to you the likes of which neither you nor that harlot wife of mine nor even I, after the fact, would have enjoyed. But I'm more concerned about my soul than you are about yours. And now, with these few words, I forgive you everything. Now stand up and face me."

Since he had not yet finished, Giacoppo said, "You have to wait to hear four words and with them you'll help me to be forgiven for this sin by God." Giacoppo told him that he would have to go to bed with his wife.

Francesco responded, "I haven't promised you this. I don't want to be like you, a wicked rogue and traitor.

Bad enough that I've forgiven you such a truly great insult. Don't argue with me because I do not want to hear anything more. Again I'm telling you to stand up and face me because nothing worse will happen to you."

Giacoppo, more frightened than before, stood up and went back again to speak to the friar. He told him how things had gone, and when he told him that Francesco refused to go to bed with his wife, the friar said, "Oh, you haven't accomplished anything because if you don't restore his honor in this way, it will be as if you've done nothing at all."

Since Giacoppo didn't know how he could return to face Francesco again, he said to the friar, "It might be better if you send for him to make him understand how it's not a sin, while I stay here. Perhaps he'll agree to do it for you if not for me."

The friar said, "That's a good idea, but I don't know him. I'll leave it to one of my younger colleagues. Point out Francesco to him from afar, and this way it won't seem that I've sent him to do this."

Going along with this, Giacoppo left with the younger friar, and pointed out Francesco to him, and the younger friar gave Francesco the message. Without any other signs, Francesco went into the church, found the friar in a little hallway in front of his cell, and pretended to have a great argument with him, but meanwhile they smiled together a little about this mockery.

When they called Giacoppo, the friar said to Francesco, "We have to console this poor man, not because of your love, because he doesn't deserve it, but for the love of Our Lord Jesus. He will also be grateful to you and He won't accuse you of a sin that you commit out of love for His

name. Both Giacoppo and I will remain obliged to you
for this."

Giacoppo threw himself at his feet begging for mercy,
imploring Francesco to go to bed with his wife. Francesco
pretended to cry out of pity and said, "Alright, I agree. I
want to right this wrong and I'll do you this favor. Out of
love for you I consent to do what you ask me to, even
though it seems very hard on my conscience."

Giacoppo, completely content with this response, became aware of another problem. Now he would have to
make his wife agree. Since he trusted that his wife would
provide when she wanted to, home he went, and it
seemed to him he had found a good trick in becoming a
billy-goat. As soon as he entered his house he began a
ceaseless weeping, so that his wife would have to ask him
why he was crying. He managed his plan so well that she
instantly began to ask him what was the matter.
Giacoppo said, "I am damned and cannot save my soul."

Once his wife heard this she began to cry more than he
and said, "Alas! Oh, how could this be? What have you
done? Isn't there any remedy for it?"

Giacoppo said, "Yes, but it's so very difficult to do."

His wife responded, "Tell me. If there's something that
can be done, we will do it."

Giacoppo said, "I'll tell you. The deed that will save or
damn me is for you to do." Then he began to describe the
situation to her. When he came to the part about what
she had to do, she pretended to be very strong. And, in
short, since he needed her mercy, he knelt down and
beseeched this favor. Then, when he had convinced her,
he went off to see Francesco as quickly as he could to get
absolved, and he said, "It's set for this evening. Come to

dinner with me, and then, in the name of God, begin to help me make amends for this great sin."

Francesco, more happy than ever, pretended that he considered this a very wicked remedy and made Giacoppo see that in going with him, he would be doing him an unusual favor. Even with everything arranged, however, it seemed a thousand years before evening came, and when it did come, he went to Giacoppo's house where he ate heartily. He then left Giacoppo in the dining room and went into the bedroom with his much-desired Cassandra. And then they went to bed. Each one realized that things would be quite different if it hadn't been for Giacoppo's affair with Bartolomea.

Since it was necessary to make amends for all the remaining sins, he returned more and more times. Then the brother sent Giacoppo away to do penance in Rome, so it was a rare night that Francesco didn't find himself with Cassandra. And so these two had what they longed for. I wish it would please God to grant us all the same end.

So, the jealous Giacoppo had to beg on bare knees for Francesco to do what he desired to do more than anything in the world, so that he would be absolved of a sin for which he had already done penance. Brother Antonio's motive was to do as some clerics often do, because many times – although infinite good is the motive of some clerics – great evil is their guiding principle, because people undeservedly have excessive faith in them.

THE TWINS NICUOLA & PAOLO

Matteo Bandello

If a noble and wealthy man put himself in the service of
another man, I can only say that it would be wonderful.
But, if he were in love that would be the end of the
admiration, since amorous passion is much too powerful
and causes things to go out of control. In fabulous Greece
they believed that the gods were in love when they did all
the shameful things that they read about them. This was
to help them understand that when a man lets love sub-
due him and lets amorous passion pierce his heart and
take root there, he can say that he gambled and lost his
liberty, and then it's not an accident if he makes a
thousand mistakes.

Now you might think it a great thing if a man were to
submit himself to love, since a man doesn't need to be
afraid that anyone will find fault with what he does
whether good or bad; but then what would you think if
you heard that a girl did the same and, dressed as a page,
unrecognized by her lover, went into his service? I think
that the woman's actions would seem more amazing to
you than the man's.

But to move on with my story, I suggest that all of us
here in this sweet and honored company will remember
that the Germans and the Spaniards so shamefully sacked

Rome in the year of Our Savior 1527. Even though the sins of that city deserved punishment, those who plundered, especially the Christians, did wrong, even if, from what I understand, most of them were Lutherans, forced converts, and Jews. But nevertheless, they behaved themselves much worse than Turks, and they committed such horrible and disgraceful acts against God and His saints that they're never remembered without pure grief. But it was not long before there was vengeance for this since, after four years, I don't believe that there were two or three thousand alive at most, out of the twenty-five to twenty-six thousand infantrymen who committed such violence in that city. The Duke of Bourbon of the French Royals, the subject of François, first king by that name in that realm, the greatest man who ever was, turned against his king and put himself in the service of Emperor Charles of Austria. He was the first to suffer the penalty for the sin that he had committed since, as Captain General of the Imperial Army, he was miserably killed by an arquebus before he could rejoice at seeing Rome taken. Most of the plunderers and robbers stole sacred as well as secular things; they were desecrators of the sacred Marian virgins and, as it is said, they were enemies of the faith of Christ. Nevertheless, those they conquered could hardly prevent the sacrileges, incests, rapes, homicides and other wicked crimes, and they could only think that, because they had profaned the religion, many would be condemned. You know of course, don't you, that after the great Pompey, an excellent man, desecrated the Holy Temple of God in Jerusalem, he lost his grandeur and never accomplished anything comparable to his many previous triumphs?

But where am I going? We weren't discussing this, and I haven't come here to weep over the ruins of Rome. But I've promised to tell you a story, and what I want to tell you is that in Rome, when it was taken from the impe-rials and everything there was sacked, a marquis from Esi was taken prisoner. This man, my compatriot, was called Ambrogio Nanni, and he was a man of honest wealth and was one of the fairest merchants. When his wife died, he was left with two children, a boy and a girl, both born in Rome. Both of them were beautiful beyond belief, and they were so like one another that when both of them were dressed either as a boy or as a girl it was very dif-ficult to distinguish them. The father himself couldn't tell them apart when, sometimes for amusement, he made them dress in one way or in another. Since they were twins they were even the same size. Ambrogio made sure they could write, play instruments, and sing, and grow accustomed to as many good things as suited their age.

When Rome was plundered they were about fifteen years old, perhaps a little more. The boy, who was called Paolo, was taken prisoner by a German, a brave man who was very highly esteemed in his country. Since he had taken other valuable prisoners and had drawn great sums of money for their ransom, the German found that they earned him gold, silver, many precious and valuable gems, and luxurious clothing. He left Rome and went to Naples taking Paolo with him, treating him like a son. In Naples, the German sold the clothes and most of the silver that he had won, and he exchanged it all for money, leaving the keys to it all with Paolo.

The girl, whose name was Nicuola, fell into the hands of two Spanish infantrymen, and she was lucky. Since she told them that she was the daughter of a rich man the two comrades treated her decently because they hoped to get a large ransom. Ambrogio saved himself with the help of some of his Neapolitan friends who were in the Spanish army. He wasn't taken prisoner, and he found a way to save his money and silver by burying them in his stable. Everything else in his house, though, was stolen. He searched, then, for his children, and he found Nicuola. He ransomed her with 500 ducats of gold. But, despite every effort, he was never able to learn anything about Paolo.

He found himself suffering the worst longing, and his grief over Paolo's loss can't be compared to any of his other losses, although they were great. Finally when he had done everything he could to find his son he worried terribly that the boy might have been murdered, since no new word came to him from anywhere about him. He had been longing to leave Rome for some time, so in bad spirits and sad beyond measure, he returned to Esi. There he put his house back in order, but he didn't want to devote himself to shop-keeping any more since he was very well-off both in possessions and in money. So he settled up with everyone as best he could.

In our city there was a wealthy citizen named Gerardo Lanzetti, a great friend of Ambrogio who was a widower. He saw Nicuola's beauty and fell deeply in love with her. Not long afterwards, he asked her father if he could marry her. He didn't care that she was very young, and he himself was much closer to sixty than to fifty, and he said he'd be satisfied to take her without a dowry. You see what this traitor Love does when he enters the breast of these senseless old men? Using their eyes he so excites them and clings to them that they make the most outrageous mistakes in the world. You see this every day. In effect, almost all the old men who take girls for wives go on to be cuckolds. Ambrogio thought it would be a pity to give Nicuola to an old man, but he didn't say yes or no, since he still hoped to have Paolo back, and he didn't want her to marry before then. In Esi, Nicuola was famous for her beauty, and no one spoke of anything except this. Every time she left the house, everyone pointed her out, and many people passed in front of her house just to see her.

Eventually it happened that Lattanzio Puccini, a young man without a mother or father who was very wealthy thanks to the blessings of Fortune and who hadn't yet passed twenty-one, saw Nicuola, and she saw him. And together they fell in love with one another. Lattanzio couldn't concentrate on anything but seeing her every day and showing her his love. How he was consumed with love for her! She always smiled whenever she saw him, and when the youth realized this he was sure that she loved him, and he thought he was the most contented lover who ever was. Nicuola found Lattanzio more handsome and charming than anyone else she knew. She was so attracted to him that the flames of love burned in her soft and delicate breast and she didn't know how to live without seeing him. Of course, it rarely happens that when two lovers desire the same thing they don't manage to get what they desire, so Lattanzio found a way to write to her and to get answers back from her. Finally, they arranged a meeting so they could talk together.

However, Ambrogio had some business that compelled him to return to Rome and to stay away from home for many days. Because he didn't want Nicuola left without decent companionship, he sent her to one of his cousins in Fabriano who had a wife and daughters. She left so suddenly that she didn't have a chance to tell her lover about it. Ambrogio left and went far away to Rome. Lattanzio heard that Ambrogio had gone and was certain that he had taken his daughter with him. He tried to find out if this were true, but he couldn't find out anything for certain, and he began to despair and was left in a very bad mood. But since he was a noble and attractive youth, he didn't stay that way too long before one day he saw Gerardo Lanzetti's daughter. She was a very beautiful and pleasant girl, and the sight of her extinguished his memory of Nicuola and relegated her completely to oblivion.

The sorrowful Nicuola, in contrast, lived in the worst grief, since she left Esi so quickly that she hadn't been able to either write or send a messenger to say good-bye to her lover. She did nothing but lament and think constantly about Lattanzio day and night. And one hour seemed to last a thousand years while she waited for her father to come and bring her back to Esi, so that she could see that man whom she loved more than her own eyes. Since she was in Fabriano at her uncle's house, Nicuola could never find a way to write to Lattanzio. Her uncle was an austere and rigid man who didn't think his daughters should be at liberty to speak with anyone who wasn't well known to them and he didn't want them to go dancing here and there. Instead he thought that they should devote themselves to their womanly tasks. Her cousins always kept her with them. They thought that she was melancholy because her father was away and consoled her the best they could.

Poor, disconsolate Nicuola was in this most painful state for about seven months, since her father found it very difficult to return from Rome, but finally he came to Fabriano to pick up his daughter and take her back to Esi. To her it seemed as if she had been brought back to paradise from hell, and cheerfully she went with her father, as you can well imagine. But once she returned to Esi, her joy changed to painful tears and fierce jealousy. Her sorrow was so deep that she almost wanted to die because she discovered that her lover was engaged with something besides combating the Jews. What made matters worse was that he seemed to remember her about as much as if he had never seen her. I'd like to have here now those girls who so easily believe the words of those youths who are like the potter's ass, which leaves an offering from his end in every door. I would show them – forgive me, you young men who are here – that out of a hundred women, ninety-nine are left deceived.

The impassioned Nicuola was in this position, and though she could easily write and send messengers to Lattanzio to try to revive the memory of their past love and what had happened between them, it was all in vain. Now she felt intense grief, and because amorous worms of the heaviest grief gnawed voraciously at her heart, she resolved to say and do whatever was necessary to recover her lover's lost grace or she'd give up her life, because it seemed impossible to her to allow him to love anyone but her.

In the midst of all this, her father again found that he had to return to Rome, but since Nicuola positively did not want to go back to Fabriano to her uncle's house, her father put her in a convent with one of her cousins, Sister

Camilla Bizza. This convent was, at other times, regarded as among the holiest. In the convent Nicuola didn't hear discussions of the lives of the holy fathers or tales of their abstinence and virtuous works, but instead all day they told each other outrageously amorous tales, and they weren't at all ashamed to say to one another, "This is my intention" and "such a man stayed last night with such a woman," and she was both shocked and scandalized. Then she saw that instead of sackcloths they all wore against their soft skin shirts of the finest cloth brought from beyond the mountains. They wore the finest clothes and, not satisfied with their natural beauty, they polished and embellished their faces with make-up and mixtures of a thousand distilled waters, musks, and powders. There was never an hour in the day that they weren't gathered in intimate discussions with various young men of the city. Nicuola, a woman who had believed that all nuns were saints, was shocked at them as they behaved so brazenly. As she got to know each one and finally when she knew them all she realized that all of them were amorous and passionate. It seems to me that any father who put one of his daughters in a convent like this must be mad, since they should be called bordellos rather than convents. But in our city, a short time after a scandal occurred, they took away all the nuns who lived there, with the pope's permission, and made them reform the place, so that ever since they've lived piously.

Lattanzio often came to this convent to do charitable work for them, stitching their shirts and other clothes. And, one day, Lattanzio called sister Camilla. When Nicuola heard him she felt her flesh burn like a fir tree that was totally on fire, and then, in the next moment an intense cold spread through her limbs. Whoever was paying attention at that point would have seen her turn a thousand colors, since she was entirely transformed when she heard her lover's name. Then she hid herself where she could see Lattanzio and hear him without letting him see her. And so it happened that Lattanzio often went to the convent and she, at her usual place, watched him and listened to him while he bitterly lamented that his page from Perugia had died at his house from a long fever. He said that the boy had served him for three years and had served him as well as one could imagine. He truly seemed very sorry to have lost him, and he said that if he found another boy like him he would consider himself very fortunate.

When he left, it occurred to Nicuola — you can see that love had conquered her — to dress up as a boy and put herself at her lover's service. But she didn't know how to go about getting men's clothing for herself, so again she felt her spirits sag. She knew one lady, her wet nurse when she was an infant, whom she told about her love. She came to the convent to see her every day. When Ambrogio left, he begged the nurse to visit his daughter often and, if Nicuola wanted, to bring her home from time to time, and the nuns knew this. Nicuola asked her wet-nurse to come to see her, and she told her exactly what she wanted to do. Although Pippa — that was her name — tried very hard to persuade her that this was madness, and she showed her the risk and the scandal that it could easily cause, she couldn't convince her. And so, Pippa brought her Nicuola home where she could dress herself like a poor boy, in the clothes of Pippa's son who had just died.

Since there was no reason to wait, the very next day, Nicuola, no longer a girl but a boy, went to the district where her lover lived. There she was quite lucky since Lattanzio was all alone up in his room. When Romulo – as Nicuola now wanted to be called – saw him, she took courage and began to wander through the district, exploring here and there as foreign boys do when they arrive in a place they don't know. When Lattanzio saw Romulo wandering around so, he thought that he was someone who hadn't been in Esi very long and who, by chance, was looking for a master. And so, when Romulo arrived in front of Lattanzio's door, he said to him, "Boy, are you from here?"

Romulo replied, "Lord, I'm Roman, a poor boy," and she told the truth because she was born and raised in Rome. "I've been wandering because I lost my father in the sack of Rome, and my mother has already been dead for many years. And since I don't know where I'm going I'll put myself at anyone's service. They wanted me to slaughter she-mules and horses, but since I'm not familiar with country life, I didn't know how to do it. In Rome I served a master as a page very well, and I took care of him and his bedroom, but during the sack the poor man was wounded and thrown into the Tiber where he drowned. When I wept for him, a Spaniard who was a forced-convert gave me a lashing and I was very badly hurt."

"If you want," Lattanzio said, "you can stay with me to serve me. I'll gladly retain you, and if I'm satisfied with you I'll treat you so that you'll always be pleased."

"Lord, I'll stay here," replied Romulo, "but I don't want anything from you other than for you to reward me

according to how well I perform my duties." So she en -
tered Lattanzio's house and devoted herself with such
diligence, skill, and polish to serve him that in a few days
he forgot how much he missed the boy from Perugia.
Lattanzio was quite pleased and proud that he had found
the kindest, most virtuous and discrete page that there
ever was. He dressed Romulo gallantly, and from among
many of the clothes he had, he dressed him from head to
foot in white. Nicuola considered herself very happy and
felt as if she were in paradise.

Now, as you've already heard, Lattanzio ardently loved
Catella, the daughter of Gerardo Lanzetti, and every day
he walked in front of her house, showing her how ardently he burned for her. Even though she would smile at
him, Catella really didn't care that much for him. She
hadn't yet exposed her breast to the flames of love. He
had sent her letters, messengers and messages, but no firm
replies, either good or bad, came back since the girl hadn't
come to any particular decision. Fortune had blessed her
father, making him very rich, but he was greedy beyond
belief. He didn't keep any servants in the house except a
decrepit old lady who was born in the house before him, a
young maid-servant, and the young son of one of his
laborers whom he always took with him. So Catella was
free to sit at her window and talk to anyone she liked,
since the good old lady kept a continuous watch at the
hearth. The girl had many suitors but she favored
Lattanzio because he had corrupted her with gifts. So as
long as he liked, Lattanzio could keep courting Catella
with messengers and letters, which he did because he
loved her beyond measure. And since Romulo seemed to
be a beautiful orator, Lattanzio taught her everything he

wanted her to do to succeed, and he sent her to speak with Catella. Romulo knew where Catella's house was, because she had passed it many times before, and she knew the maid, because she had seen the master speak to her a few times.

And so she was given this errand and went entirely against her will, as unhappy as one could possibly be. But before she went to find Catella, she went to Pippa's house and said to her, "Oh, mother, I'm the most desperate woman in the world since I haven't dared reveal myself to my lover, and since I see how fiercely he is in love with Catella Lanzetti. My love makes me so unhappy that I can't see how any good can come of this. And what's worse and torments me even more is that now he is sending me to speak to her for him, and to persuade her to love him, because he will ask her father for her hand and will marry her. Now you see, mother, where I'm headed, and Fortune can do nothing worse to me than what she already is doing now. If Catella is prepared to love him and is satisfied to have him as her husband, I won't live another hour. I can't see any possible escape from this tormented life of mine, because it's impossible for me to live seeing him with another woman. Tell me what to do, dear mother, and help me in my urgent need.

"I still hoped that when Lattanzio saw how I treated him he would discover one day what I had done and would be persuaded to have pity on me. But now all my hopes are gone with the wind, because I know that he is fiercely in love with that woman and all day and night he never thinks or talks of anything else. Help me! If my father comes back and finds out what I've done, what will happen to me? He'll kill me, certainly, and no excuse would be of any use. Dear mother help me, help me by God, dear mother!" The whole time Nicuola cried desperately.

Pippa, who loved Nicuola more than her own daughter, was touched by her weeping and began to weep herself, but she dried her tears, and then said to her, "Look, daughter. You know what I've told you many times about this love, and you never wanted to believe me. It certainly seems best to me if you stayed away from him. I'll take you back to the convent until your father returns, and I'll arrange the matter so that everything will be okay, because if he finds out that you, dressed as a man, served Lattanzio and slept in his bedroom all those nights, what do you think he would say about your behavior? I guarantee you that you would never find a husband, and even though you swear to me that no one recognized you as a woman, I don't believe you. You can say whatever you want, since I'll believe what seems reasonable to me, and what one must believe. I know what these young masters are used to doing with their pages. Therefore it would make me happy if you'd take care of yourself, get this whim out of your head and devote yourself to someone else. At this point your father can't stay away much longer, and I wouldn't want him to come now or know anything of these stories for all the gold in the world, since it will be bad news for you and me! If you see that Lattanzio wants Catella and every day you can touch with your hand how much he is in love with her, why do you exhaust yourself in vain? Why do you want to put your life and your honor at so much risk if there isn't any reward at all to have from it? All difficulties demand a reward, and it's folly to endure this labor in vain, especially when so much harm might follow. And you, what reward do you expect for so much servitude? You await eternal infamy, not only for yourself, but for all your family and, since it's not a small matter, you might even lose your life. Why love someone who doesn't love you? Why follow someone who shuns you? I myself was never so mad that I wanted to run behind anyone. Leave that man, daughter, and turn your thoughts somewhere else, since in this city there's no lack of young men equal to you, who'll love you and take you as their wife. How do you know that this man, even if he still hasn't recognized you until now, might not recognize you one day and take from you whatever he wants, and then not care for you any more, and act so that you become a woman of the common herd, pointed out as a shameless harlot? Listen, my daughter, to this advice and stay here with me."

Nicuola lingered a bit on this thought and then, after a fervent sigh, she said, "My dear mother, I know that you speak with love, but I've already done so much that I must see it through to the end, whatever might happen. Now I'll go to speak to Catella and I'll see which way she's moved, because until now Lattanzio hasn't had anything but general replies from her. Then, God will help me, since he knows my heart and he knows that I didn't do this for any reason except to have Lattanzio for a husband. I'll want to speak with you here every day, and if my father comes, we'll arrange our affairs as best we can, because it's no use for me now to worry about trouble before it comes."

Then she left Pippa and went away toward the Lanzetti house, and she arrived just as Gerardo entered the piazza

to do some of his business. Catella's maid was in the
doorway, and Romulo made a gesture to her that she was
sent by her master. She was brought in and put in one of
the ground floor bedrooms. The maid went upstairs and
said to Catella, "My lady, come down, because Lattanzio
has sent his very handsome page, whom you've told me
you like so much, to speak to you." Catella quickly de-
scended to the bottom of the stairs and went into the
room where Romulo waited for her. When she saw
Romulo, she thought she was seeing an angel, so handsome and graceful did the page seem. Romulo began,
after paying her respects, to say everything she had been
told by her master. Catella felt an intense pleasure
listening to her talk. She gazed lovingly at her, and it
seemed to her that from her beautiful eyes came an
unusual sweetness, and she died with a desire to kiss her.
Romulo concentrated on telling her about Lattanzio's
interest, but Catella heard little of what he had to say,
being intent on staring at her, and saying to herself that
she had truly never before seen such a handsome young
man. She gazed at the page so lovingly, and Romulo's
beauty and good grace so overwhelmed her that she
couldn't restrain herself anymore, and she threw her arms
around Romulo's neck and affectionately kissed her on
the mouth five or more times. Then she said, "Does this
seem like a very good idea to you, to bring me these
messages and put yourself at the risk you would face if my
father found you here?"

Romulo clearly knew then that Catella was in love
with her and saw her turn a thousand shades of red, and
she answered, "My lady, anyone who stays with someone
else and serves must do these and similar things according

to his master's will and command, and I for myself do this very unwillingly. But since my master wanted it, I also want it. However, I beg you that you'll give me a welcome reply and have compassion for my master, since he's your servant and loves you so much, so that when I return to him I can cheer him and bring some good news."

They talked a bit together, but nevertheless it seemed to Catella that the page's good looks became even greater and, when she thought that the page had to leave her, she felt shooting pains in her heart that pierced through her, and so she decided to expose her passion and said, "Upon my faith in God, I don't know what you've done to me, but I'm certain that you've bewitched me."

"Lady," she replied, "You deceive me. I haven't done anything to you. I'm not bewitching nor enchanting you. I'm your good servant and I beg you to give me a favorable reply, because you'll be the reason for my master to hold onto his life and to hold me more dearly than he has before."

Catella wasn't able to suffer any longer, since she was pining to kiss the page again, and she said, "Look, my life and heart of hearts, I don't know a youth in the world who would have made me do what I have now done with you, but your good looks and the infinite love that I've had for you since I first saw you following your master have driven me to this. I don't want you as a servant but rather, if he won't miss you, I want you to be my master, as long as I live, and I want you to have me at your disposal to fulfill your every desire. I don't ask who you are, or if you are poor or rich, or who your family is. My father, thank God, is wealthy enough for you and me, and so old that he can live only a little longer. Devote yourself to your own affairs and let Lattanzio go, since I will never love him and I will begin, starting today, to stop smiling at him."

It seemed to Romulo that necessity would follow its own path, and after some further discussion she promised Catella to do whatever she wanted. She would thank Lattanzio without end for his offer, making Catella eternally obliged to him, but she would have to do it carefully so that Lattanzio wouldn't catch on to anything. They talked together and decided what Romulo would tell Lattanzio. After many loving kisses, Romulo left relieved of a great fear that she had at times that Catella might have put her hands in places that would have told her that Romulo was not a man. She left then and went away to Lattanzio's house and found him anxiously waiting for her. First she excused herself for her delay saying that she had to wait a long time before she could speak to Catella. Then once she was able to speak with her, she discovered that she was in a terrible mood because that very same morning her father scolded her very sharply for this love of hers, and yes, also because her father heard that Lattanzio was in love with some other girl. Romulo said, "I tried very hard to get this idea out of her head, and I gave her a thousand reasons and argued with her for a long time, but all of it was in vain."

Lattanzio was left very bewildered and in a bad mood at this news, and he made Romulo tell and retell at least ten times all the words that passed between Catella and her. Lattanzio then asked Romulo to go back and speak to Catella as soon as she could to assure her that he didn't love any woman in the world but her, and that he would offer every possible proof of this to her. He wanted her to know that he would do just as she wanted, since he never loved another woman, and he was ready to be her eternally most faithful servant. Romulo said she would do everything she could, and she went to talk to Catella.

The following day, Catella was at the window when Lattanzio passed through the quarter, and when he arrived near the house, the young woman rose from the window with a disdainful gesture and went inside. This led Lattanzio to believe what Romulo had said when she warned her master. Lattanzio returned home in the worst mood possible where, with Romulo, he began to lament his disgrace and bad fortune. Moved by his anger he said that Catella was not the most beautiful woman in the world nor the most noble, and that she shouldn't pride herself so much and scorn him. He had a great deal to say on this matter. Romulo began very skillfully to tell her master that these things often occurred either because of indignation or scandal mongers or because two people have different opinions, since it's clear that very often a man will love a woman who would never yield love to him, and another woman will love a man who wouldn't consider loving her.

Lattanzio said, "Romulo, you tell the truth as it is, and the pure truth. In these past months one of the most beautiful girls in this city who had just arrived from Rome loved me, and I know that she wished me all her best, and I loved her very dearly. But she went away – I don't know where – and stayed away quite a while, and during that time I happened to see this splendid Catella, so I abandoned my love for her, completely turned my shoulder on her, and cast her into oblivion, and then I devoted myself to serve this ungrateful woman. The other woman finally returned to the city and sent me letters and messengers, but I didn't care about her."

"My lord," Romulo said, "it serves you right, and you've received the return that you deserve, because if such a beautiful girl loved you as much as you say, you've done wrong without end to leave her for this woman who, without knowing it, avenges the other woman. A man ought to love the woman who loves him and not follow the one who runs away. Who knows, perhaps this beautiful girl still loves you and lives for you in misery? Many times I've heard it said that girls love their first loves much more tenderly and fervently than do men. My heart tells me that this unhappy girl must still pine for you and lead a distressed and difficult life."

"I don't know," said Lattanzio, "but I do know that she loved me intensely and that she's very beautiful. Compared with her, Catella seems almost ugly. Furthermore, I must tell you that many times it's occurred to me that if you were dressed as a woman I'd say that you could be her, since you resemble her so completely, and I believe there's little difference in age between you and her, though it's true that she was somewhat bigger than you. But let's speak of this thief Catella, whom I can't get out of my mind, always thinking about her day and night, I can't turn my heart from her toward another. Tell me. Will you dedicate your heart to speaking to her and to revealing my love to her completely?"

"I'll do what I can," replied Romulo, "and even if I were sure to suffer death over this, I'd return to her."

🦌

Now we'll leave these people to these plots of theirs for a little while and speak of Paolo, son of Ambrogio, since without him we can't finish our story.

At this same time Paolo's German master left Naples and arrived at Acquapendente en route to Lombardy, and from there to his homeland. While waiting to leave Acquapendente, he became sick with a violent colic, which after three days took his life. But before he was at death's door he realized he was dying, made his will, and left Paolo heir to all that he had. Paolo arranged an hon-orable burial for his master and paid the innkeeper. Then he set out for the fork in the road toward Esi where, a little while before the fall of Rome, his father had sent him to stay for about a month. When he arrived at Esi, he didn't go straight to the house as he had planned but went with his carriages to the inn. There he arranged to have his baggage unloaded, and he asked the innkeeper to watch and guard his things. He cleaned up, left his com-panions at the inn, and set out all alone to go around the city. Because he had made a vow to dress all in white, he was dressed the same way that Romulo was.

Paolo went to see if his father's house was open, and on his way he passed in front of Catella's house. She was at the window, but he didn't acknowledge her, because he didn't know who she was. The young woman was very surprised by this, because she felt certain that it was Romulo, and she quickly sent her maid to call him. It was the hour of nones, and few people were in the street when the maid called Romulo and said, "For pity's sake, come back here. My lady calls you." He realized that he was being called by mistake, and he was even more sure of it since the maid spoke to him as if they had known one another for a long time. For this reason he decided to see who this woman was. Thinking that she might be the wrong kind of woman he said to himself, "Let me go try my luck since with me she won't be able to get anything, unless I give her an extra coin or two."

Now, just as he was going toward the house Gerardo arrived at the top of the street and, when the maid saw him she said, "Romulo, you see who's coming. Go on your way. Get out of here."

He went off, noticing first, however, which door the maid opened, and who the man was who entered the house. The maid locked the door, pretending not to have seen her master who, walking very slowly as old men do, didn't notice her. Gerardo came and knocked at his door and, once it opened, he went inside. Paolo observed the house very closely and saw Catella at the window. She appealed to him beyond measure, and because she seemed very beautiful and graceful, many thoughts went through his mind.

Then he turned toward his father's house, which he found closed with the windows locked, and so he thought his father was not around. Nevertheless, to be more certain about it, he asked some tailors who had their shop there, what they knew of Ambrogio Nanni. They told him that it had been a while since he was seen in Esi. Paolo returned to the inn with various thoughts still running through his mind about the girl he saw. He wanted to go back to see her, and he wondered whether he ought to go alone or to bring along some of his dead master's servants, whom he still retained. He decided not to go, but instead stayed at the inn.

Meanwhile Ambrogio returned from Rome and met Gerardo on his way home. After welcoming him, he said, "Ambrogio, you've come in time since if you had been here a few days ago, I think we would've concluded your daughter's marriage to me, or at least it would be clear to me whether you wanted to give her to me or not, because I've decided not to wait in doubt any longer."

"As you can see," replied Ambrogio, "I've just arrived, and I'll stay here for some time. We'll get together and speak about this at greater leisure."

As they were discussing this between them, Ambrogio on horseback and Gerardo on foot, Romulo, who was trying to return to speak to Catella — since Lattanzio had imposed it on her — saw her father and went off in another direction. She went to find Pippa and said to her, "Alas, mother, I'm dead, because my father has returned and I don't know what to do with myself."

"Come on," said Pippa, "have faith in God! Don't leave the house and leave everything to me. Take off these clothes and dress in your own, which are here in my house." Pippa immediately went straight to Ambrogio's house. Right at that moment, Ambrogio was getting down from his horse. With a happy face Pippa greeted him saying, "Welcome sir, a thousand welcomes. How are you?"

"Oh, hello, my Pippa," replied Ambrogio, "Where are you going in such a hurry?"

"I've come straight to you," she answered, "so that I could take care of whatever you need, because Giannelloccio Bindi told me that you were coming, and I don't know if these relatives of yours know how to cook."

"Thank you," said Ambrogio, "But it wasn't necessary for you to take such trouble. I've sent for Margarita, who used to stay in the house, and she'll be here on hand to work. But tell me, how long has it been since you've seen our Nicuola?"

"I see her every day, sir," replied Pippa, "And just this morning I stayed quite some time with her. She was dying for you to come back. I've often brought her to my house and kept her there two or three days. She's really a good and beautiful daughter, and she works marvelously with her hands, as God knows." In the meantime Margarita arrived, and she began to do the housework. Pippa stayed a good while with her, helping her. The hour seemed to last a thousand years as she waited to leave, and finally she said, "Sir, with your permission, I'll go this evening and get Nicuola from the convent and bring her with me to my house. Then tomorrow I'll bring her here, or better, I'll keep her a day or two with me, until you've arranged to put your house in order."

"Do as you like," replied Ambrogio, "And give my regards to Sister Camilla as well, and kiss my daughter for me. Go quickly." Pippa left and before she went to her house she went to the convent to speak with Sister Camilla. They arranged everything that was needed for Nicuola's safety in case Ambrogio might go to the convent. Sister Camilla, who was a good mistress of such crafts, told Pippa not to worry, since everything would go well. Pippa left the convent and went to her house where Nicuola, who was no longer Romulo, waited for her, dying to hear how things went. She was already dressed in her own clothes and she had fixed her hair as girls usually do. When she returned, Pippa told her what she had done and told her that if she wanted to go home to her father the next day, or stay one or two days it was all right.

Nicuola decided to stay the following day with Pippa, and she did nothing but torment herself over Lattanzio. Her longing to have him for her husband couldn't be greater. Pippa kept her, as she promised, and tried to get her to think about something else, but clearly her hard work was in vain. She knew that Lattanzio was so in love with Catella that he never thought of anything else and, in the end, he would get what he wanted by asking Gerardo for permission to marry her.

"This is what torments me," said Nicuola. "And whenever I think about it, it makes me despair. If only my father hadn't come so soon, I bet that I would have put Lattanzio into such disgrace with Catella, that she would rather have had a peasant for a husband. But my father's sudden and unexpected return has ruined everything."

"It's ruined everything?" replied Pippa, "Instead it's fixed everything. If what you've told me about what has happened between Catella and you is true, I advise you that you were headed toward the worst end, since if you went back there to speak to her another time, without a doubt, after some kisses she would've wanted to play with her hands, and finding you a girl, what do you think she'd have thought of you? The two of you would have been left in perpetual shame. Don't you think she would have quickly assumed that you were Lattanzio's harlot?"

"This is what I wanted to happen," added Nicuola. "As you say, she wouldn't have known that I was Nicuola, Ambrogio's daughter, and she would have come to hate Lattanzio so much that never again would she have been able to see him or hear his name. This is how I could have regained his love."

Pippa couldn't contain herself but laughed at Nicuola's arguments, and she said to her, "Daughter, put your heart at peace. If it's ordained by God that Catella must be Lattanzio's wife, all the crafts, talents, and skills that you know how to use will be of no value to you in disturbing such a marriage. You're still a very young girl, beautiful and rich, since one has to believe that if your brother Paolo were alive, we would have heard something of him by now. But the poor boy must certainly be dead, so our lord God has taken his soul. So if you manage yourself wisely, you'll be left the sole heir of your father, and so you won't be without a noble and wealthy young marquis. So get these fantasies out of your head that do more to bore you and bring you pain than pleasure or reward."

While these things were going on, Paolo decided to go alone to see Catella, and late that day he passed in front of her house but, since he didn't see her, he went back to his inn and decided not to go out anymore for that day. Lattanzio was becoming extremely aggravated waiting for Romulo, and when he saw the night darken he was very surprised that she didn't return to the house to give him an answer and tell him how things had gone with Catella. Since he had waited an hour, then two hours into the night for Romulo to come without seeing him, Lattanzio was left in very bad spirits and worried that Romulo might have had some misadventure. But he couldn't imagine anything for certain so he lingered almost all night without sleeping, with various thoughts running through his mind. Certainly he loved Romulo very much, because she served him very well and she was discrete and virtuous. Also she never argued with anyone in the house, but diligently took care of whatever she was given to do. And so when he thought he had lost her, his love grew wonderfully again inside him.

As for Catella, who fervently loved Romulo and had already tasted his sweet kisses, she wanted to come to closer grips with him, and because she hadn't seen him again after Gerardo came home – having mistaken Paolo for Romulo – she went off in a very bad mood to lay down. Nicuola discussed Lattanzio all night with Pippa. Sighing and tossing, she didn't sleep herself and didn't let Pippa sleep either. Since she knew that Pippa had told her father that she might stay a day or two, she decided to stay with her a little while longer.

In the morning, since Romulo hadn't appeared at his house, Lattanzio sent people to search for him here and there and to keep an ear peeled on the streets to see if anything was known of him. He made arrangements for people to spy everywhere, and he gave them a description of Romulo's dress and age. One person said he had seen him the day before entering the house of Pippa Di Giacomaccio who lived near the cathedral. Lattanzio, who knew her, heard this almost at dinner time, and he went to find her and knocked at the door of her house. Pippa went to the window and, recognizing the youth, she was surprised and worried that perhaps he might know that Nicuola was in her house. She said to him, "Young man, who are you looking for?"

"Mona Pippa," he replied, "When it's not a bother to you, I'd like to have a word or two with you."

"Twenty-five," said Pippa, and telling Nicuola that Lattanzio was below, she hurried downstairs and opened the door. The young man entered the house and sat near Pippa in a place where Nicuola, without being seen, could see him and hear whatever he said.

Now Lattanzio began to speak, saying, "Mona Pippa, though I've never done any worthy favor for you that gives me hope to presume to ask you any kindness and have it, nevertheless it's my custom to be kind to every-one. I know you are a woman who is loved by many gentlemen who consider you to be courteous, so it gives me the courage to appeal to you with the firm hope that you will completely satisfy my wish. Therefore, without further ceremony, I beg you affectionately to tell me what is this that I hear about a boy dressed in white who came here yesterday to find you? His name is Romulo and he's about seventeen years old. He has a very handsome and gentle appearance, and he's my page. He hasn't returned to my house since yesterday. I beg you – for goodness sake – please tell me what you know about this. This way I'll be satisfied and always obliged to you."

"My son," said Pippa, "thank you for the good and courteous kindness that you show me. It's certainly very dear to me as well, and I'm happy that you've come yourself to my poor house, because for several days I've wished for a chance to speak with you, which now you've given me by your courtesy, and which I don't want to lose. Before replying to your inquiry, I should tell you that I don't know how to give you an account of this boy of yours because neither yesterday nor for many days before has there been any boy here or any young man that I know of. And certainly I would know if he had been here."

"Perhaps you're afraid," added Lattanzio, "that I might punish the page for not coming back to my house. But I promise you, with as much faith as I have that I won't give him any trouble, provided that you tell me the truth about why he didn't return to me yesterday."

"Don't worry about that," replied Pippa, "because there's no man in this house, and there wasn't one here yesterday. It hurts me terribly that I can't help you in this, which I would willingly do." While Pippa reasoned with him, Lattanzio sighed. Finally she said to him, "Young man, you appear to be head over heels, and there's no person, hearing these ardent sighs, who wouldn't think that you were too much in love with your page. But I've also heard that you loved a beautiful girl. Don't lead me to believe that now you're an enemy of women."

"For pity's sake" said Lattanzio, "I wish to God that I weren't in love, since then I'd be more cheerful and content than I am. And you shouldn't think that I mean this about my page, since I'm not thinking of him. I'm speaking of a young girl whom I love much more than my own eyes and much more than my soul." When he said this his grief filled his eyes with hot tears, and some even wet his cheeks, and still he sighed bitterly.

It seemed to Pippa that now she had the opportunity to try everything that she had already planned, and she said to him, "I know too well, my son, that what you're telling me has to be true. You've proven that you're in love, and I believe that your pain has to be great, because I'm of the firm opinion that there's not a pain in the world that's sharper and more painful than to love some-one and not be loved in return. I know that the young lady whom you love doesn't love you at all, but now she hates you since she loves another more than you."

"And where did you hear this Mona Pippa?" Lattanzio asked her then, full of surprise.

"Don't ask how I might know it," she replied. "It's enough for you that I know that now you love someone who doesn't love you, and it has not been so many months since you loved another girl much more beautiful than this one, and I know that she ardently loves you. I also say this: she loves you now more than ever, and you love her neither more nor less, but you don't remember her anymore; it's as if you'd never seen her."

"I don't know what you're saying," said Lattanzio, "but since you've guessed the truth so well and it seems that you know my business so well, for goodness sake, tell me how you know that the one I love, now doesn't love me but loves another."

"I can't tell you this," replied Pippa, "because it doesn't seem proper to me. It seems right, however, to remind you that it serves you right that you love someone who dislikes you, since you scorned the young woman who loves you. This is how God punishes our sins and deep ingratitude. And if nothing worse happens to you it won't be so bad. For pity's sake, think of the poor unfortunate Nicuola, who loves you and whom you have loved! She certainly did the greatest things in the world to win your favor and all has been in vain. And you Lattanzio, you love Catella more than yourself, and she doesn't care for you at all. Now go, follow this through since in the end you'll see your error, and perhaps, when you're ready, you'll amend your ways."

When the young man heard these details he was almost beside himself and he didn't know how to reply. On the other hand Nicuola, who heard and saw it all, would also have willingly gone out to say a few little words and speak her mind about her case, but she decided to wait and see what end these discussions would reach, and so remained quiet. Pippa also waited to hear what the young man would say. Then, almost as if he had awakened from a deep sleep, he said, "Mona Pippa, I want to speak with you at length since you know my circumstances better than I do. It's true that I loved Nicuola Nanni, and I know she loved me. Then her father sent her away from the city, I don't remember where, and so during that time I began to love Catella, daughter of Gerardo Lanzetti, who pretended to love me for a while. But now, I don't know why, I've discovered that she is entirely reluctant and totally against my wishes so that if she's in her doorway or at her window when I pass by in the street, she goes inside as soon as she sees me, and she doesn't want to hear any more from my messengers or receive my messages. Just yesterday I sent my page to see if he could speak to her, but he hasn't returned to give me any reply, so now I find that I've lost both my lover and a good and very kind servant. If he had returned and told me that she was still adamant in what has become her usual cruelty, I was ready not to bother her any more, but to find myself someone else who would be willing to accept my attention since, to tell the truth, it seems madness to me to follow someone who runs away from me, to love someone who doesn't love me, and to want someone who doesn't want me."

"Wonderful. Then you understand what I'm telling you," said Pippa, "and certainly I wouldn't be mad enough to love someone who doesn't love me. But tell me please, if Nicuola still loved you, rather if she loved you more than ever, what would you say to that? Would it seem to you that she would be worthy of your love?"

The young man replied, "She would be worthy for me to love her as much as myself. But what you say can't be true, since she must be, and I am reasonably certain that she is, angry with me, because she's written to me many times since she returned to Esi and I simply didn't pay any attention to her. Now I don't even know where she is, it's been so long since I've seen her."

"Oh," said Pippa, "I know that you saw her and spoke to her in a very familiar way several times just a few days ago."

"You're wrong about this, Mona Pippa," replied Lattanzio.

I'm not wrong," she answered, "because, in truth, I must know what I say. I don't speak to the wind. But tell me, if what I tell you is true, and with your own hand I could make you touch Nicuola who loves you more than ever, what would you do? And if she might have stayed in your house and served you, and done what every menial servant must do, and was never recognized by you, what would you think? What I tell you shouldn't seem strange. Don't pretend to be amazed, since it's true, and it can't be anything other than what I say. And so that you can see that I've told you the truth, I'm ready to make you see it in such a way that you'll say what I say. But first tell me, if Nicuola did everything as I told you, what would she deserve?"

"You tell me fables and dreams," replied Lattanzio, "But if that were true, I wouldn't know what to say except that I'd have to love her immeasurably and make her my mistress."

"Good," said Pippa, and she called Nicuola, telling her that she should bring the clothes of the page that she wore. When she heard this, Nicuola, who had heard everything, took the man's clothes, and stood before her mother and her lover, her face all flushed. Pippa said, "There, Lattanzio, is your Nicuola. Here's your Romulo, here your so-very-longed-for page who was beside you day and night and who for love of you placed herself, her honor, and her life in the greatest peril. Here's the one who, scorning the entire world, cared for you alone. But never, in all that time, did you recognize her." So she told the entire story of how Nicuola was transformed from a girl into a page, and she asked him, "What do you have to say to me?"

Lattanzio was stupefied. He gazed at Nicuola, and he seemed entranced. He didn't know what to say about the fact that she had stayed with him dressed as a page. When he recovered a bit and thought of Catella's cruelty and that Nicuola was very much more beautiful than Catella, he weighed her love, and the risk she had taken because of her extraordinary love. Almost weeping he said, "Nicuola, I don't want to hear these confusing stories about what you've done. What a mess! But if you're inclined the way Mona Pippa says you're inclined, and if you're willing, I'd like you to be my wife."

Nicuola, who wanted nothing else in the world more than this, found herself feeling so much joy that she almost couldn't contain herself. She threw herself at his feet and answered, "Merciful lord, since you agree to marry me, here I am, ready to serve you always. I will be yours forever, heart and soul."

Then Lattanzio drew a ring from his finger, took her for his legitimate spouse and wed her in front of Pippa. Afterward he said, "So that we carry this out with higher repute and greater honor, as soon as I've dined I'll go speak to your father and ask him if I might marry you. I'm convinced that he'll give you to me without an argument. Then we'll arrange our wedding as it suits him."

To put the seal on the words of the marriage agreement, Mona Pippa arranged that Lattanzio and Nicuola would lie together in one of the bedrooms and consummate the sacred marriage before he left. Both of them were marvelously satisfied with this arrangement. Then Lattanzio, putting everything he intended to do in order, left and went to dine, and after dining he found Nicuola's father. Nicuola went home with Pippa to find her father, who happily received her.

Meanwhile, Paolo had left the inn as soon as he had dined and began to go toward Catella's house alone. When he reached the end of the street, he saw Gerardo come out of the house and go, I don't know where. Gerardo was scarcely gone when Catella appeared at the window and saw Paolo and, believing that he was Romulo, she called him in since he was near her door. He resolved to discover what this was all about, so he went in, and in an instant Catella came downstairs, embraced him, and amorously kissed the young man that she believed was Romulo, saying, "My life, dear and final end of my every thought, you still make yourself too scarce. You don't yet love me as much as I love you. I also told you, my heart, two days ago, that I don't want anyone but you for my husband. Let's go here into this bedroom." Then she told her maid to watch in case her father returned and warn her if he did. Then, she started kissing Paolo wantonly, saying very sweet words to him and biting him playfully. It seemed that she would lan- guish in his arms. He, who was absolutely no fool, perceived that he had been mistaken for someone else, and pretending to be completely impassioned and almost mute from such intense love, kissed her over and over and sighed.

"My soul," she said, "I'd like you to break away from your master so that we can be together whenever we like."

"Don't worry about that," replied Paolo, "I can certainly find a way to be free of him."

"Yes, my life," said Catella, and still she hugged him to her breast and kissed him. Paolo, who was young, was entirely prepared to please her, and feeling himself grow- ing like the grass in the meadow, he put his hands over her bosom and sweetly felt her breasts which were still those of a girl, small, but as round and firm as two apples. Since she wasn't at all reluctant, he took somewhat greater risks. He began to play with his hands in all those parts where the pleasures of love find their true satisfac- tion. Catella, for her part, was quite inflamed with passion and excited to find herself in the arms of such a handsome youth. She felt a pleasure that she never felt before, and she let him do what he wished.

Paolo took that occasion, joking and playing, to throw her on a little bed and made her taste a sharp sweetness while he broke the first lance. But then, in the battles that followed he knew so well how to do it, that he broke four more lances with so much pleasure for the girl that she wanted to joust many more times. They didn't realize how many hours had gone by, and the maid went to do her work around the house leaving the door open to the street. At this point Gerardo came home. He passed in front of the bedroom where the lovers, exhausted from the match, had sat on a bench to talk. He heard them and said, "Who's inside?" In a flash he asked the question, moved his feet toward the door, and opened it.

When he saw Paolo with his daughter, he was sure that it wasn't Paolo but Nicuola with whom, as I've already said, he was quite in love. So he forgot how angry he was when he came in, thinking that Catella might be with a man, and he looked at Paolo. The more he looked at him the more he was sure that he was Nicuola. Catella was left half dead when her father appeared, and Paolo trembled all over, but when they saw that the old man stopped himself, they said nothing for a while and waited with courage to see how this would end. As I've already said, Paolo and his sister Nicuola were so very similar that even one with more practice had the greatest difficulty telling which of them was male and which female. Gerardo, then, looked at Paolo for a good while with the greatest admiration, and since he knew that Ambrogio's son hadn't been found he was certain that this was Nicuola dressed as a man, and he said to Paolo, "Nicuola, Nicuola, if you weren't who you are, I assure you that I would've played a sad trick upon both you and Catella."

Then he turned to his daughter and said that she should go upstairs and leave Nicuola behind, because he would make better company for her than she. Catella left, and it seemed to her that things had gone well until that moment, since her father had neither scolded nor struck her. But she didn't understand, nor could she possibly guess why her father called him Nicuola.

For his part, Paolo was worried that the old man would want to do the same thing with him as he had just done to his daughter, and he said to himself, "This mad old man might want to try the impossible, but things won't go as he believes."

When Catella left, Gerardo said, "My dear Nicuola, what kind of dress is this I see you wearing? How could Ambrogio, your father, let you go out like this by yourself? Tell me the truth. What have you come here to do? Have you, perhaps, come to see how I keep my house in order and how I live? It's been two days since I spoke with your father who had just arrived in Esi. When I asked him if he wanted to decide if he would give you to me for my wife or not, he told me that he'd speak with me later. I assure you that you'll have good times with me, and I'll leave you to rule the house." He said that she wouldn't have anything but good treatment from him.

Paolo said to himself, "I've certainly been taken by mistake twice today. The daughter of this man believes that I'm a certain Romulo of hers, and he thinks that I'm my sister, but his daughter is certainly not confused about that part."

Gerardo continued to say, "Nicuola, why won't you say anything to me? Tell me what you think, and I'll arrange it all."

He wanted to kiss him, but Paolo drove him back, and said to him, "If you want anything, speak with my father and let me go. I don't know why I've come here."

The old man who believed he was Nicuola said, "Go on, go, since I'll speak to your father and I'll bring an end to this matter."

Paolo left and went to his father's house where he met Lattanzio who had asked Ambrogio for Nicuola as his wife. Since Ambrogio knew that he was young, brave, and rich, he promised her to him. When Paolo entered, Lattanzio saw him and was left dazed, and if Ambrogio had not, at that moment, made him hold hands with his daughter, Lattanzio would have thought Paolo was Nicuola. I can't describe the immense joy Ambrogio felt when he saw his son, since he thought he was dead, and his joy grew even greater because he had not only recovered his son, but he had honorably married his daughter.

There were many embraces and great celebrations among those four. While they ate breakfast, Gerardo arrived, and he saw Nicuola playing with Lattanzio, and Paolo, whom he thought was Nicuola. He spoke with Ambrogio and, almost unable to contain himself, he said, "Lord help me! I don't know if I'm asleep or if this is really happening to me." And crossing his hands he was left all full of amazement. Paolo, who supremely enjoyed the savory kisses of Catella, said to his father that he'd be honored to marry Gerardo's daughter. Ambrogio, who knew he would be a good relative, told Gerardo that he had married Nicuola to Lattanzio, and he begged him to give Catella to Paolo for his wife, so that this other marriage could be settled.

And so, happy beyond his every hope, Ambrogio found that he had recovered his son, rich and well married, and also that he had married his daughter very well. Paolo arranged to move his people and his things from the inn, and he kept two servants for himself. He discharged the others so that they were quite happy. Everyone was full of joy except Gerardo, who still wanted Nicuola. Yet in the end he gave them peace. The two lovers and their wives devoted themselves to having a good time, and such is still the case today.

AN ASS TRICKS THE BROTHERS OF MODENA

Matteo Bandello

🐎

I've always been convinced that nothing in the world is truly worthy of praise or truly deserving censure or truly neutral. The same is true for the story that I'm about to tell to you here above this grassy and cool shore of the clear Lambro. You can't help but find a useful and pleasant lesson in this story. Listen to me, and you'll hear about the venerable monastery of San Domenico in Modena, where Friar Agostino Moro da Brescia, whom everyone knows, is the prior.

On the third Sunday of Easter, a very good and excellent preacher, who had preached all of Lent to everyone's satisfaction, took a bit of freedom with what ordinary preachers are accustomed to do during those ceremonies in that monastery's church. Everyone throughout the city knew that this preacher would be preaching his last sermon, and so many converged on him that it seemed as if a plenary indulgence was being offered in that church. The throng of people was so great that the church was scorching hot just from so many men and women breathing. So when the sermon was finished – it lasted from after dinner until almost 10 o'clock – the friars said their vespers and evening prayers together with great difficulty. The sacristan, who was a clever man, opened all the windows to air out the church, and he went outside and waited until later so that he could lock the large door. Afterwards, that very same night, they had to bury an evil man who had a very wicked reputation. Everyone said you could see the devil at work in him, and they all believed that he'd be taken away in spirit and body. Once this wicked man's funeral was finished, the sacristan fastened the great door of the church, but he left the door that led to the first cloister open so that the church could cool off better during the night.

That very same night a friar who had preached in the mountains arrived. He carried all his things on a little ass as black as pitch, which he left to rest in a little stall. After everyone had gone to sleep, the little ass left the stall – I don't know how – and went into the cloister where the grass was tender and fat, and he stayed in the cloister a long time grazing on the greens. Later then, perhaps after he got thirsty, he went sniffing all around, and he came upon the font of holy water which he drank, as the friars would realize the following day. When he was satisfied with his eating and drinking, he went and sat on the grave of the wicked man who was buried that evening, which was all covered with sand. There he trammeled around many times, and then he laid down to rest.

When matins sounded, the novitiates went to the choir, as usual, and prepared the candles and books for singing the service. At matins, then, two young men went to pre-pare things, and as they passed through the door of the sacristy to go the choir, they saw Mr. Ass stretched out on the grave with eyes that looked like two great burning coals and two large ugly ears that stood out like two horns. In the dark, and already afraid of the one who was

buried there, they saw the beast, who looked quite dreadful at that hour. The frightened young men lost all sense
of judgment. Without thinking any further, they believed
that beast was the devil. They were so scared that they
ran away as fast as their legs would carry them, thinking
that the one who ran fastest would be most fortunate.

When they reached the dormitory, panting and almost
unable speak, they met some friars who were going to the
choir, and among them was the master of the novitiates.
With the light that burned all night in the dormitory, he
could see that they had turned back, and he asked them
why they hadn't gone to prepare for the service. All
excited but with nervous voices, they told him that they
had clearly seen the enemy of human nature on the grave
of the man they buried last evening. The good master,
who wasn't the bravest man in the world, began to tremble with fear and stood between two other friars, afraid
that he might fall.

At this moment Fra Giovanni Mascarello arrived, a
chorister and superb musician who, after he heard about
this, courageously went down. When he entered the
church and saw that beast who had stretched out its ears
because of the clamor, the friar thought he was standing
in front of the dead man and his wicked life. He quickly
turned his back, locked the door to the sacristy, and ran
the whole way back screaming as loud as he could,
"Fathers, it's the devil, the enemy of us all!" He repeated
this over and over many times. He has, as you know, a
very loud voice and he shouted so loud that there wasn't a
friar in the monastery who didn't hear him.

The prior, who then had come out of his cell, stood in
front of Fra Giovanni and he asked, "What madness is

this? What did you say? Are you crazy or something? Keep quiet and don't make such an uproar at this hour. What has gotten into you, in the name of God?"

"Father," the singer replied, "I'm not crazy, but I tell you that the devil's in the church, and I saw him clearly with my own eyes on the grave of the man we buried yesterday evening who had such a bad reputation. I believe that he's come to carry off that man's body with him to hell. These two young men have also seen him."

When the prior asked them what they saw, they said the same thing that Fra Giovanni had said. So the prior with some of those friars who had gathered there because of the uproar went down and into the church. Since all of them only knew what they had just heard, and they only saw with their imaginations, when they cast their eyes upon the ass they thought without a doubt that they were seeing the infernal demon. So all of them, frightened as could be, made the Sign of the Cross and returned to the sacristy where the prior, consulting the fathers who were there, sounded the alarm. When all the friars had gathered he encouraged them, telling them to keep up their spirits and not be frightened by the diabolical apparition. The friars then all went together into the sacristy where they dressed in sacred vestments and took all the relics they had. Once everyone had a sacred object in his hand, they left in a procession with the cross in front, devotedly singing the *Salve Regina*.

Through all this Mr. Ass, who continued to relax on top of the grave, wouldn't move at all from there. Few of the friars were daring enough to raise their eyes toward the beast, since they all believed that devil was there, not an ass. The ass didn't get up after they finished singing the

Salve Regina, and when the prior requested the book of exorcisms used to drive evil spirits from the bodies of the possessed, he read everything that would be suitable under similar circumstances. The ass still made no sign of wanting to get up. In the end the prior took the sprinkler of holy water, and drew even nearer to the ass, lifted his hand, and began to make the Sign of the Cross by sprin‑kling the ass with holy water. Because of the image he had fixed in his mind, he never perceived that it was an ass and not a demon.

Now, either because he had drunk his fill of holy water or because the water was cold or perhaps because he was worried he might be hit with the sprinkler, after seeing the prior lift his hand several times as if he wanted to hit him, Mr. Ass got up on his feet and with a horrible asinine roar, which he blared with a great voice, he began to groom himself, as he usually did. With his tail lifted high, he made twenty-five balls of dung and soiled the entire grave. These ridiculous acts proved to the prior and the friars that he was not the devil but Mr. Ass.

All those good friars were left holding their noses, and they didn't know what to say or do. In the end, every‑thing was resolved with a great laugh, and it seemed fine to them that everyone, young and old, philosopher and theologian, should be humiliated by the sight of an ass. Certainly you can say that an active imagination of wicked things causes a great deal of harm, and that it's better to investigate the truth with a reasonable amount of courage rather than rashly give in to fear and someone else's fantasies.

GONNELLA TRICKS MARQUIS NICCOLO D'ESTE

Matteo Bandello

🦂

Gonnella was a Florentine, the son of a Master Bernardo who kept a shop where he made boots, purses, laces and other things from leather, and because he led a commendable life, he was often elected rector of the laudists of Santa Maria Novella. Because he didn't have any child but Gonella, he sent him to school and raised him very properly. The youth was very capable, and he learned grammar very well, but he was inclined to play pleasant tricks on everyone so that everyone thought he was very charming.

He didn't like his room in Florence and liked the craft that his father practiced even less, so when he was about twenty years old, he went to Bologna without asking permission from his father. But he only stayed a short time because, when he heard about the famous Marquis Niccolo, he decided to become one of his courtiers. He went to Ferrara where he arranged everything so very well that he became a servant of Marquis Niccolo with a good salary. He hadn't been at court very long when, with his charms and with his jokes, everyone already loved him so that even the Marquis began to love him – but not in a vulgar way – and to show him in many ways how dearly he thought of him. The Marquis grew used to him and in a short time he was so familiar with Gonnella that it seemed as if he wouldn't know how to live any more without him.

Gonnella was perceptive, cunning, and confident in his speech, his opinions, and his suggestions, and whatever he proposed, he always confirmed it with some undeniable justification. His Tuscan speech was also very eloquent so that he could persuade anyone about anything. I remember that I heard my grandfather, who said he knew Gonnella when he was still a courtier, say many times that his buffoonery and pleasantry didn't come from either madness or stupidity, but from the vivacity, acuteness, and sublimity of his genius, since everything he did, he did deliberately. When he decided to have some fun, he considered the type of people he wanted to trick and the possible pleasure to the Lord Marquis. Of all the tricks that he played at different times, I want to tell you about one that he played on the Marquis.

Gonnella was by nature very pensive. Because of this, whenever he was alone, he always dreamt up and imagined some pleasantry, and he would first plan it three or four different ways before he put his hands to work. So one day, after he had decided to play a joke on the Lord Marquis, he sat at a window of the palace that opened onto the piazza facing the bishop's church. He had a little knife in his hand and often, lifting his eyes to the sky he made certain ciphers and characters on the wall with the point of the little knife. The Marquis came up to him, and Gonnella pretended not to notice him and continued making his letters, lifting his eyes toward the sky and, with his hands making thousands of little gestures, so that it seemed that he was deeply immersed in the most important thoughts. Then, after the Marquis waited long enough to observe those eccentricities a bit, he said to Gonnella, "What is this, are you crazy now?"

When he heard the Marquis, he pretended that he hadn't noticed him before and said, "May thirty demons descend on you at once for coming here!" He pretended to be very irritated and said, "I'd pay quite a bit if you hadn't just now distracted me, since an infinite number of instants have passed in the course of the heavens while I was calculating something, and I'll need time before I can go back to where I was. Go, for the love of God, and don't drive me crazy. This is a fine thing, that I can't have two hours a day to do what I want! Where is Gonnella?" Gonnella asked then. "Make him come here at once. When I come, then I find that there's nothing."

The Marquis then said, "Oh, you see, what a good joke! This is one of those jokes that you know how to make. What whim do you have in your head? What madness? What astrologies? Your spade won't enter my soil."

"I'm off!" added Gonnella, "I'll yet find myself a little place where you won't come to disturb me, because if you knew what I was doing, you wouldn't have broken the spell for me."

Then the Marquis had the greatest desire in the world to spy on him and to see what he was up to, and right then he began to beg Gonnella to reveal what he was doing. Then after he let him plead and plead for a good long while, Gonnella said, "I was making an astrological figure and it was almost finished but you, with your arrival, have ruined it all for me, because God knows when I'll find myself disposed again to decipher these astrological chimeras."

"Oh, oh!" said the Marquis. "I know that these are some of your tricks and pranks that aren't worth anything. Where did you learn astrology? I'm sure you're delirious, big lunatic that you are."

"I tell you, I've told you and I'll tell you again," replied Gonnella, "that you will live with me a hundred years and still not know the one-thousandth of my powers. Go, go away and don't bother me. Yet, you'd do better to learn this beautiful and delightful science since it still ought to be very useful to you, and it's very easy to learn. I'll oblige myself to teach it to you in no time."

The Marquis left without doing anything else. Gonnella then began to make characters and symbols every day, sometimes with a pen on paper and sometimes with the little knife on the wall. He managed to put them where the Marquis would see them. When he noticed this, the Marquis decided that he still wanted to see where this would lead. Gonnella knew the names of the planets and was acquainted with many stars in the heavens, and so, one day, speaking in the presence of the Marquis and his physician, he said some things – I don't know where he learned them – that related to the influence of the heavens on human affairs. He said this in such a way that the doctor, who wasn't the most learned man in the world, thought that Gonnella was the perfect astrologer. Then the doctor turned to the Marquis and said, "Sir, that man is in league with the devil. He's not what we thought. My lord, he's just touched on certain points, which in astrology concern extremely obscure doctrines."

Because of what the physician had said, who must have been a close relative of Simone Da Villa, the Marquis began to believe Gonnella's fibs. Gonnella realized this and plotted a better way to trick him and give himself some amusement. He arranged that the physician would be the one who was tricked, the one made the wet knight like Maestro Simone was. Now, listen how.

It's usual, almost customary in Ferrara, that there are often many loads of bowls, plates, tankards, earthen pots, pans and other terra cotta vessels carried about by asses on the public street near the loggia, which is below the great palace of the court, since they sell them as housewares there. Gonnella met with one of these vendors and arranged that on a certain day, he would come by the narrow little street that leads into the piazza toward the saddlery shop with a number of pots. Because his ass was accustomed to the walk, the vendor would lead him to another section far from where he normally unburdened the ass and would drive the ass through the piazza along the front of the cathedral. When they reached the door of the temple, pretending to be anxious and deranged, he would break the stoneware and kill the ass, and run off. Under penalty of the disfavor of the Lord he was never to tell anyone who put him up to this. In Ferrara, Gonnella was well known by great and small alike, and everyone knew how much the Marquis liked him. So the earthenware vendor, well paid for the earthenware and for the ass, very gallantly carried out at the appointed time what Gonnella had asked.

Now, the day before the assinicide, Gonnella sat at his usual window with his usual instruments, and he was not there long before the Marquis appeared and approached him. Gonnella pretended to be quite impressed by what he appeared to comprehend of the signs and characters he made. Then, he turned to the Marquis and, pretending at the same time to feel regret, admiration, and I-don't-know-what sort of sorrow said, "My Lord, be well advised by what I tell you now, and don't ignore what I say, since if my art doesn't deceive me this time, you soon will have results that'll prove my art is true. Tomorrow in the piazza I see a great conflict between two people, and in the fight I see that one of them will die with a great deal of blood from many wounds. But as yet, I haven't been able to figure out the hour or how to stop it, but I am sure that it'll happen tomorrow."

The Marquis heard him speak with such certainty and heard him predict the day of the dispute, and he replied to Gonnella, "From now until tomorrow isn't a long time. We'll certainly see these miracles of yours and see if you chatter on without knowing what you're talking about, or if indeed you're telling the truth. And if these prophecies don't occur, I want you to sound the trumpet, and I'll make you spread the word throughout all of my state that you're the greatest liar alive, and I'll make you publicly confess that you're an extremely ignorant fellow and that you know nothing."

Gonnella answered him saying, "And if, my Lord, you find that I'm truthful, reason certainly requires that I be rewarded."

The Marquis replied, "If you've told me the truth, I'll have you crowned astrologer laureate with wonderful privileges."

When the next day came, the earthenware vendor appeared, according to their arrangement, and after he broke all of the pots and gave the ass a fierce thrashing, as Gonnella wanted, leaving the ass horribly wounded, he despicably cut its throat with a sharp knife and left it to die on the ground. He then went away to attend to his affairs. An uproar arose in the piazza and everyone raced to the scene to see the vendor, acting like a drunk or a madman, give the animal a furious caning with a stick. There wasn't one person who ventured to approach or rebuke him for fear that he'd give them a similar thrash-ing. The event was quickly reported to the Marquis. He turned to Gonnella, who was with him, and said, "By my faith, you're certainly a poor astrologer at this point, be-cause instead of a great fight with one person dead, as you predicted, the affair has involved the death of an ass."

Gonnella, appeared to be astonished and said, "My lord, one slight point of error in the calculations is the reason for these false judgments, but I want to go back and calculate anew to see where the flaw lies." Although the thing didn't work out as Gonnella had predicted, the Marquis still thought he was very skilled. He decided to put himself to the test to see if he could learn this art of prophecy, and he agreed to Gonnella's proposal. Seeing his chances go from good to better, Gonnella said, "My Lord, I venture that, before fifteen days have passed, I'll be able to give you such principles that later, by yourself, you'll be able to prophesy. But I need to sleep in your bedroom during this time, and your physician, who spoke so well of me, must come with me."

The lord was indeed pleased. At nightfall, Sir Gonnella woke the Marquis and the physician, and he showed them first the star of Jupiter and then Venus and the other planets along with the Bear and other constellations. The

Marquis learned these things very well in only a few days. The physician spat out a round of praise because it seemed to him that Gonnella was a great astrologer. Gonnella ordered five pills from an apothecary that clear out the body without doing it any harm, and since it seemed time to set fire to the mortar, he took all five in one night which, around midnight, began to stir his system. Gonnella heard that the physician slept with his belly up and snored with his mouth open, so he got up quietly and silently turned his ass round to the physician's face and with a great roar of his belly he relieved himself of the bad news on the physician's face, and more than seven drams fell into his mouth. The poor physician, all covered with filth, woke up and wanted to scream. He was forced to swallow a bit so that, with all his noise, he woke the Marquis, who smelled the stench, and heard the physician's complaints and said, "What the devil are you doing? Who has let one loose?"

Gonnella, who had already left his bed said, "Marquis, you see that I've satisfied my duty and I've made you an astrologer, because suddenly, at midnight, without light and without any calculations you divined the truth from the very beginning, because the physician is full of shit."

Then he called some servants, and made them take the physician away wrapped inside his sheets. The Marquis then said, "Gonnella, Gonnella, this has certainly been one of your best tricks, but you stink too much." And he returned to sleep.

JEALOUS IOAN TORNESE

Masuccio Salernitano

🦗

In the time of our most illustrious lord Duke Filippo Maria de' Visconti, there was in Milan a graceful and noble knight named Sir Ambrosio de L'Andriani. He was a rich, handsome and virtuous youth, and because of the magnanimity of his uncommon spirit, this man yearned to see the natures and deeds of the Christian princes. He explored many places both inside and outside Italy, and he finally heard of the great splendor of the court of your King Alfonso and of his continuous triumphs that made his memory immortal in the city of Naples. He made up his mind and, to satisfy his yearning, he decided to see this court as well. He put thousands of florins in a purse, and with his horse and with attendants trimmed in noble attire, he went off to Naples.

There he saw the dignified districts and remarkable parts of the city, and he realized that the renown of the city was not diminished by his presence. For this reason and the one that first led him there, he proposed to stay, enjoying himself and having a good time for as long as his money would last. He became familiar with a few gentlemen from Capua and he went with them now and then, to celebrations, masses, and tournaments, where crowds of women gathered. He considered the women carefully and said to his companions that the Neapolitan women, in his judgment, were endowed with more presence, grace and feminine worth than with overwhelmingly abundant beauty.

He was in the middle of this discussion when one of his dearest companions, a young nobleman named Tomaso Caracciolo, agreed with the knight and added, "If fortune gave you a look at a little woman from Nola, who is the wife of a shoemaker called Ioan Tornese, I've no doubt, according to everything I've just heard, that you'll confess that she's the most beautiful woman you've ever seen in all of Italy. But the way that her husband keeps her seems impossible to me. He holds her shut up so that no person, not even a relative, can see her. Because of his unheard-of jealousy and his suspicion of the Duke of Calabria, and because of the renown of her great beauty, he doesn't trust her. Nor should he trust her. If what my maid, who is one of his neighbors, told me is true – I don't know if I believe it – you will hear these strange things. Apparently he never wants to leave her alone in the house, so everywhere he goes he always takes her with him dressed as a man. So, free from worry, he allows the people of our land to see the greatest beauty. Therefore, if you wouldn't mind, I'd like to try to see her."

Without another word they set out together for the shoemaker's workshop, and when they arrived there Tomaso said, "Master, can you make a pair of new shoes for Sir Ambrosio?"

"Of course," he responded. "At your service." And he gestured for the knight to enter, while he sat himself on a little bench and began to fit him for shoes. Tomaso, who was trying to stall for time, turned to them and said,

"Now I'll go to take care of an errand nearby while you're being fitted for shoes."

With this excuse he departed, leaving the shoemaker to begin the fitting. The shoemaker worked with his head bowed, which this work required, while Sir Ambrosio raised his eyes and turned to look all around, since all his thoughts were fixed on seeing this beautiful woman. It was his great fortune that focusing his eyes through a little crack, he saw a woman who was staring at him from down in the shop. Because he had enough time in the shop to see her very well, he looked at her for some time and finally saw that a rare and inestimable beauty showed in her countenance. She seemed to him to be adorned with even more excellence and shapeliness than Tomaso had told him. So, during the long delay that the shoemaker needed to give him a good fitting, he not only had the chance to gaze at her carefully, but he also had the chance to make affectionate and sweet signs to her as if he infinitely burned with love for her. The young woman, who was very prudent, knew that because of her husband's extreme caution, she wouldn't be able to satisfy herself, and even though the graceful knight endeared himself to her by showing her how much pleasure she brought him, she decided not to show any positive sign, and the fitting finished in such formality.

After the knight paid the shoemaker he said to him smiling, "Truly I've never worn shoes which, in my judgment, I could say fit so well. And yet if you'll make me a pair every day, I'll pay you the same price each time."

The shoemaker, very glad for his good luck, felt he was fortunate that such a truly gallant and magnanimous knight had arrived in his workshop. He figured that he would make a great profit from him and responded, "Go in the name of God, and I promise to serve you always as best I can."

In the meantime, Sir Ambrosio returned to Tomaso, delighted that good fortune had granted him so much right at the beginning, and he told everything to him, confirming that the woman had the most memorable face that anyone had ever seen, but that he didn't see the rest perfectly enough to make a judgment. He begged him, in the end, to give him his prudent counsel about this. Though Tomaso had lost hope about it all, nevertheless, as a good friend willing to serve him, he sharpened all his wits and without leaving out a single detail, either of the discussion or the place, they went through all the possibilities that every fervent lover would think of. Finally they decided on a plan and proposed to wait until a time and place for him to carry it out with ease.

While the knight continued to buy shoes every day at the same price, the shoemaker, to entice him even more, began to talk to him like a servant, and sometimes he invited him to a light breakfast in an alcove in the back of his shop, and the knight had good reason to be happy with such entertainment.

These men continued in their newly-formed friendship, and when the feast of Saint Catherine came and the brigades went to Formello, the knight went to the front of the castle to take a stroll. Since he was staying nearby, he decided to wait to see if Ioan Tornese came to the feast with his wife dressed as a man. After a little while he saw Ioan Tornese from rather far off coming toward him with a young little scholar whom he quickly realized was the person he already thought he was. A special friend and comrade of his also accompanied him. When the shoe-maker was asked who the young man was, he said, as he had many other times, that he was his brother-in-law from Nola, a student in medicine, who had arrived here to visit his sister. As they engaged in these discussions, ev-eryone tipped his hat to the knight wherever he strolled, and he returned their greetings. He looked closely at the scholar and recognized him as the one he waited for with supreme desire. He asked the shoemaker with a smile where they were going. He said that they were going to Saint Catherine's. Sir Ambrosio began to walk with them, and along the way said, "I was also going to go and, as always, I was waiting for one of my servants or someone else I knew to go with me. But since no one has come, I'll go with you."

They set out together and reached the place where the feast was being celebrated, and since the place was crowd-ed with a throng of people, the knight sometimes had the opportunity to squeeze the young scholar's hand and to let her know that he recognized her. He was answered by a similar sign since she knew him very well, so it seemed to him that he'd succeed with his plan, and he was more than happy. Having come so far so early in the game, he made arrangements with his host and sent all his servants to do errands, so that no one would be around until late, and then he'd wait for them when the feast was finished and return home with them.

When they arrived in front of his inn, he took Ioan by the hand and began to speak in this way: "My dear sir, you've invited me many times to dine with you and you've honored me in your house, so it seems right to me, even more so since I'm a guest here, that you and your companions stay to have breakfast with me this morning."

Although Ioan didn't lack prowess like timid men, he was a very jealous man, as you know, so he found it very difficult to allow his wife to eat at the inn, even if she were dressed as a man. He declined the invitation many times but, in the end, he was forced, mostly by his dear companion's persuasiveness, to accept the invitation so they would not upset his friend the knight. They went up together over a little archway where there was a nicely laid table, and the knight quickly summoned the host and asked him where his servants were. He said that they had gone to the market to buy fodder and forage for the horses. He pretended to be upset about this, and he said, "Even if all the servants were hung by the throat, we'd certainly do what we came here to do. See to it that we have good things to eat."

Just as they had arranged, the host told him, "Sir, I've nothing delicate prepared that might suit you."

"Why not," asked the knight? "Lazy scoundrel, suddenly I'd like to dig your eyes out. I have here more than 200 florins to spend, and just now that I've brought my friends with me, who've shown me a thousand honors, you're not ashamed to say that you don't have anything?"

"Don't be upset, sir," he responded, acting quite timid, "since you'll be served as if you were the King."

The knight turned to him in a rage and said, "Now go away, brute that you are, and get to work at once to roast me the best goose you've got."

The host left to make quick delivery of that order, but the knight remained huffing. He was consoled by the others to have patience, and he expected that, in any case, he'd be able to make excellent servants of them. The knight thanked them and said, "Besides the failure of the host, I'd like to hang one of my servants when he comes back, since he left me all day today as alone as you see me now."

Ioan, who didn't perceive the plot, both to humble himself and to show himself willing to please said, "Do you want anything? We also consider ourselves to be your servants."

The knight answered, "I consider you brothers rather than servants, but I'd like a little of the hot sauce that you call mustard. Without it I won't be able to eat the roast this morning. One of my servants knows a place to buy it where it's good – I believe it's in the Old Market. Since I don't have that servant to send for it, I can't do anything but rage against him."

Ioan regretted his offer, because he would have to leave his wife for such a long time that his heart would ache, but he prepared to go and held his tongue. The knight knew this, and he turned around again to face him and said, "Well, sir, if it's not a heavy burden, could you take the trouble to go yourself for this sauce, since with it, our meal will be excellent."

Poor little Ioan was very unhappy because it seemed a dishonor to deny such a small request, and he couldn't think of any obvious reason to bring his wife along. He couldn't think of doing anything but what he was asked. He approached him, completely entrusted his scholar to him, and taking a bowl, he set off flying for the mustard.

The knight saw him leave, turned to the guardian, and said, "Oh, I've forgotten the most important thing."

"What do you need?" he asked.

The knight said, "I wanted some oranges, but because of my rage I forgot to tell Ioan."

The guardian replied with true faith, "I'll go quickly to get some, since I've some of the most beautiful oranges in the world in my shop. Just yesterday they arrived from Salerno."

He left quickly while Sir Ambrosio remained alone with the woman, according to his preconceived plans, and considering that there was no time to lose, he took her by the hand and said, "And you Sir Doctor, here you'll understand one of my secret afflictions." He dragged her into the bedroom and approached the bed with the same sensation known by all who have uniquely felt that desire, and with the swiftest wings he took one good flight. He had hardly finished when the companion returned with the oranges and found the bedroom door locked. The two lovers had just given each other such wonderful delight when the companion put his eye to an opening in the door and saw that after the fact, the knight held the youth in his arms and gave her many secret and sweet kisses. The guardian felt great regret, and with contempt he drew back, realizing that the knight had achieved some wickedness with the good scholar and had become truly intimate with him while he was left in his care. He went down to the entrance where Ioan arrived. When he didn't see his wife, Ioan was dazed and beside himself, and he quickly asked where the scholar, his brother-in-law, was.

The guardian said, "I wish to God that I had bitten my tongue this morning when I persuaded you to stay here because I've lost faith in this knight, your great friend, who truly seemed to me a man of integrity, accomplished in every virtue. But now I've discovered he's a great scoundrel."

"Alas," said Ioan. "And what could it be?"

"The misfortune that God gave you!" he responded, "Since, with the same artifice that he used to send you away, he also sent me for oranges, and when I returned I found him with your brother-in-law locked in the bedroom, and through the cracks in the door I saw that he used him as if he were a pretty and charming young woman."

Ioan was neither alive nor dead when he heard this foul story but was completely perplexed and beside himself. He went upstairs and saw the knight seated at the table talking with the scholar as if nothing had happened. Flushed with rage and grief, crying and with a desperate voice he said, "By my faith, Sir, this has been a great Milanese courtesy. But after you've eaten the meat without waiting for the mustard, you'll relish the mustard without ever tasting such a dish again."

Then he threw the bowl on the table, grabbed his wife by the hand, and with the greatest fury said, "Come on, let's go, in the name of the devil, let's go home since, without having eaten, we've paid the bill and to make matters worse, I've even bought the mustard!"

He threatened her fiercely while going down the street. The companion, who didn't fully understand the nature of the injury, followed him downstairs and hounded him for having made such a uproar in front of such a gentleman because of an errand boy, saying, "What's the matter? Do you think he'll get pregnant? What's done is done. Why make such a mistake and lose a great friend for such a small matter?"

Ioan, who was intent on getting his wife home quickly, didn't care to respond because of a great rage gnawing inside him. Consequently, the good companion, who didn't want to let him make himself miserable, comforted him hoping to help mend what had been done, which he thought was really a small offense. He continued to bother him so that Ioan couldn't bear it anymore, and trembling with rage he said, "Stop it, my friend! You'll make me blaspheme God and all the court of paradise this morning. Don't you see that this is my wife?"

"How could he be?" he said. "And why do you lead her around like this?"

Weeping, the shoemaker told him the reason, and his prudent comrade at first harshly blamed him, adding, "My Ioan, you were badly advised and the right and proper penalty has followed your foolish thoughts. You're not of this world. For pity's sake! Poor man, haven't you noticed how corrupt and ruined the world is today? They watch boys more closely than women! In fact, that woman is a live decoy for falcons, and I'm amazed that this morning, as well as thousands of other times, she wasn't torn from your arm. But now that the thing's done you can complain, not about others but about your-self. You've got this problem because of your bad fortune, and it makes you take strange precautions. When God gave you a woman for a wife He didn't want her trans-formed into a man. I don't say that she shouldn't have the protection that a pretty, young wife must have, but not in this strange and unheard-of way. Anyway, they're worth little in the end because all wives are inclined to deceive their husbands, so that no one can ever be really prepared. And don't think that you're the first or the last who'll receive this blow. Haven't you ever reflected on the great masters? They always play these jokes, and they keep quiet out of prudence after they're deceived so that they don't add eternal infamy to their pain."

With this and other consolations his companion comforted Ioan till he reached the house, and he left him there, taking care that he wouldn't also be listed among the deceived. Swiftly he returned to the inn, where he found the knight with his dearest friend Tomaso. He joined in with them, and all together they enjoyed the just-completed joke and the dinner they had planned. After a long period of suffering, Ioan died of grief while his wife remarried in joy and, as beautiful as ever, delighted in her robust youth.

HOW SAINT BERNARDINE WAS TRICKED
BY TWO MEN FROM SALERNO

Masuccio Salernitano

🐉

The old men who knew him affirm that Angelo Pinto, our Salernitan, was in his day the most terrific master of deception with every rare trick, so that throughout Italy the likes of him could never be found. He traveled to many places, both inside and outside Italy, and in almost every place he employed the tools of his trade. So he arrived in Florence during the time when our most devout Saint Bernardine preached. Because of the great number of his miracles and the widespread fame of his perfect life, most of Tuscany followed this man.

One day, by chance, Angelo found himself with another young man from Salerno, who was called the Vescovone, among a multitude of people listening to Saint Bernardine preach. The Vescovone himself was a rather learned disciple, considering his age, of the science of Angelo Pinto. They recognized each other at the same time, and in memory of their native land they embraced one another and told each other about their many adventures. Finally the Vescovone said, "Angelo, I've stopped here to carry out a good joke, but I haven't yet found a person in whom I can confide, who's also well-supplied with a great number of florins."

He described the joke to Angelo, who found it extremely amusing. Angelo said that he was ready, both with the money and with the necessary ingenuity to be part of this remarkable deception.

Not lingering very long over his thoughts, Angelo took out a very large purse that contained some little bags. Into it he put 500 ducats of gold that he had left over from a much greater sum that he had already squandered. Separating the Florentine coins from the Venetian coins and placing them all in various bags according to their stamp, he made a record of everything, and put this receipt in a wallet. What he had prepared would serve the Vescovone's purposes very well, and they rehearsed the plan they would cautiously execute.

On the following morning, Angelo, with the purse to his chest, disguised himself as a pilgrim. When Saint Bernardine finished his sermon and entered his cell, Angelo followed close behind, and then threw himself at the Saint's feet asking, his grace to grant him a kind audience, since his problem couldn't bear to be delayed. Saint Bernardine kindly responded that he would listen to him, and while he wept, Angolo said, "My father, you'll hear that recently in Rome I received a plenary remission of my almost unforgivable sins, so that I was restored to the pristine innocence that was mine when I received the waters of Holy Baptism. However, as penance for my most enormous wickedness, I was sent on a pilgrimage to Saint James of Compostela. I was on my journey, and yesterday morning I purified myself here by listening to your holy words when the devil, beside himself with concern that I was being taken out of his hands, cast a noose before me, with which he would have caught me by the throat! That noose was this purse that I've found. It contains a good 500 ducats. He used this purse to show me my extreme need and made me see my three little daughters – rather pretty but badly dressed – and all at the age when they might marry. I've certainly considered all the possible perils they face because of what they lack. When I thought all this over, however, it consoled me to return and with my poor brigade to enjoy the good things Fortune had sent to me so that while I was still armed with the powerful forgiveness of the Holy Spirit I could resist such a true temptation, thinking only that no great treasure is anything compared to my soul, which God wanted to save with his most precious blood.

"With this resolve I've come to you. I beg you, in God's name, take this money and tomorrow, while preaching, tell the people about it. Then, no doubt, you'll find out who it belongs to. When he tells you what's in the purse, return it to him. If you don't think that I should take any reward from this purse with a good conscience, then I beg you to praise my poverty to the people of this city."

The glorious Saint heard what this saintly man had to say and saw the money that proved his story. He considered everything carefully, and because the man seemed old and looked respectable, he not only believed what he said, but he thought that it was an unprecedented miracle. And since the world was ruined and corrupted by the she-wolf avarice and by an insatiable gluttony for money, he never expected to find so much goodness in the human spirit.

After he praised him enthusiastically for his new virtue, he said, "My son, I don't know what else to say to you, but that, if you had crucified Christ, your goodness in doing this would have been enough to obtain pardon for you, without any further pilgrimages. But you should know that you're right to follow your judgment. Don't worry. God won't let this good deed pass unrewarded. I for my part will do my duty tomorrow, as you will see, and in such a way that I hope, with the grace of my Creator, you will, in time, have relief from your poverty. And you'll have it with a good conscience, since it was none other than the accursed enemy of God who appeared before you to make you fall into damnation."

Angelo gave infinite thanks to the Saint both for his benevolence, but more so for his offer to petition the people for him in the morning. As he left him with the purse filled with florins, he said to him, "My father, I must tell you – not to boast, but to tell you the truth – I'm actually born of noble people, and I wouldn't want to be recognized begging here. That is not my way. Tell me what I must do."

Saint Bernardine readily believed him and for this reason had even more compassion for him, and so he arranged that Angelo wouldn't leave his cell. When the new day came, Saint Bernardine climbed up to his pulpit, as he always did, changed the announced theme, and said, "He has done miraculous things in his life. Who is he and will we praise him?" Then he added, "Dear citizens, I've come upon a marvelous event, a miracle rather than a human deed. Therefore, it seemed appropriate to me to digress from the promised sermon and propose to you the theme that you've just heard. It's about a poor man who was going to Saint James for the purgation of his sins when early yesterday morning the devil came to him amidst the throngs, revealed himself, and put between this man's feet a bag containing hundreds of florins. He was tempted sorely and struggled over this because of his extreme poverty and the thought of his ruined family for which, with difficulty, he's able to give only basic sustenance. Finally, comforted by Christ's love in this and his other infinite miseries, with the Sign of the Cross he rejected the temptation. Crying bitterly he came to me and brought the purse, filled to the brim with florins, which I have now in my possession. I don't know what more Saint Peter would have done or even our angelic Francis – Christ's imitator and sole disparager of worldly things who didn't want to have anything for his own – if when he found the treasure he didn't try to return it to its owner. Therefore, even more must we praise this man, who is entangled in the world and who needs this wealth, since he is very poor and laden with daughters. Furthermore, he is a person of such nobility that shame forbids him from begging. It seems to me that it would be worthy for the church to sing the praises of this man today in the theme proposed for our prayers: 'He has done miraculous things in his life.'"

Then in a loud voice he began to say, "And you, rapacious wolves, avaricious gluttons, foul flesh splattered with mud in the deeds of this deceptive world, every day you follow the practice of usury, make false contracts and bad gains, and with your deceptions you take your neighbor's things, rob the church, usurp the power of the weak, drink the blood of the poor, fail to follow the Gospels and with thousands of other depraved deeds you deviate from Christ, following instead the path of the devil!"

And then the poor old Saint, angry and inflamed with love, finally grew tired and finally calmed down. Then reiterating the theme, he said, "Neither could I with a pen write, nor with my tongue recount the praise that one should deservedly bestow on this man. Nonetheless, I want you to heed one single aspect of his goodness and purity: Talking to me, he explained why he didn't seek a reward for the money he found, since he believes that he can't take it in good conscience. However, my followers, that man who lost this money should come to me and bring his receipts for the purse, telling both the number of florins and their serial numbers and stamps, because they are already arranged this way. Without paying a cent, he can take it away with the blessings of God. However it's up to you to comfort yourselves by following the doctrine of our Savior Jesus, who wished that, just as every evil deed is punished without mercy, just so no good deed should go unrewarded. Therefore, it seems to me, my children, that this poor man should receive some compensation for his virtue, and I think I must exhort you even more because of his poverty. I beg all of you who are blessed by the triumphant banner of the Cross of Christ, that you each throw some contribution here into my mantle in order to emulate God. However, no one should give a pittance since then we'll collect so little money from the many thousands of people I see here, that it won't be worth the trouble. Console yourselves with the idea that helping the needs of the pilgrim or of any other mendicant is for the greater good."

As soon as he threw his cape on the ground, all the people moved forward in the greatest throng that they had ever made, each one offering holy alms. The cape was held out by Saint Bernardine's companions so that throughout the day it would receive the offerings and in the evening, when they retrieved it, it had by easy count nearly a thousand florins. It was in the midst of all this that the Vescovone came forward disguised as a Genoese merchant, since he knew that language very well, and in the middle of the great throng he shouted in a loud voice, "Make room for me." Finally, in tears, he knelt at the feet of the holy brother and said, "Sir, the money's mine, and either here or elsewhere I'll politely give you the receipts for it, since I have it all written down."

He took the record, which he had reserved for this occasion, out of his pocket and handed it over. With a pleasant face Saint Bernardine said, "My son, you've had more luck in finding your money than you had sense in watching it. Nevertheless, come with me and we'll see. If it's yours, you can take it away without paying a cent."

After he gave his blessing to the people, he went to his cell and poured out the money, and when he found that it agreed with the Vescovone's receipt, he happily returned it to him.

Taking the money, the Vescovone went quickly to the place where Angelo's family was lodged and, as they had planned, they left Florence together and went to a certain place to wait for their master. The following morning Angelo was given the money, and in the presence of the Saint, he had certain bankers, who were devotees of the Saint, convert the money into gold to make the deception more complete. With his money on him he received the Saint's grace and benediction and took his leave. He went to meet his companions and together with the greatest merry-making they rode to Pisa. There they divided the spoils among themselves in a jolly mood, and each one then went on his own way. And one can imagine that they ended their days as usual: at someone else's expense.

One can say that this prank was both pleasant and artful and it was also useful and fruitful, since not only a wise saint but almost all of those astute Florentine people were deceived in a single stroke by these ordinary men.

HOW TWO ROMANS DECEIVED SIR FLORIANO OF BOLOGNA

Masuccio Salernitano

🐟

Sir Floriano of Castel San Piero was, in his day, a very famous and exceptional doctor of law in Bologna. One day as he was leaving church with certain other doctors, he strolled through the main square to the silver shop where he had commissioned a beautiful chalice of gilt silver for himself. He spoke with the silversmith, agreed on a price, and paid him. He turned around to arrange to have his attendant bring it home, but he didn't find him there, so he asked the silversmith to send his boy with it to his house. The silversmith willingly agreed to this.

Just then two young Romans arrived in Bologna from the district of Treio. They had been running around throughout Italy with forged coins, dice, and a thousand other deceitful snares to trick people, and they ate and enjoyed themselves at everyone else's expense. One of them was called Liello de Cecco and the other was Andreuccio de Vallemontone. By chance they were in the square just as Sir Floriano had the chalice sent to his house, and they saw what was happening and proposed to try to get their own hands on it.

They knew which house was the doctor's, since they watched the boy closely. Liello told his companion what they had to do. They went to a market and purchased a good eel, and Liello hid it under his cloak and took it quickly to Sir Floriano's house. He knocked at the door, asked for the lady, and when she came before him, said, "Your husband sent this fish so you can prepare it quickly and delicately, because he'll come home to dine with some other doctors today. He also said that you should send back the chalice that the silversmith's boy brought earlier, because there's been some disagreement, and he wants to return it to weigh it again."

The simple woman easily believed him and quickly handed him the chalice, then she told the maids to pre- pare the fish in a hurry, and she then made all the other arrangements for their dinner guests. While she waited happily for them, Liello, carrying the chalice, quickly went towards San Michele in Bosco where there was a Roman friar who was very close friends with them and as crafty as they were. He greeted Liello who told him what they had done, and together they enjoyed the booty. Meanwhile they waited for Andreuccio, who stayed in the square to listen for news of their trick.

At dinner time Sir Floriano left his companions and went home. His wife greeted him when he arrived, but when she saw he was by himself she asked, "Lord, where are the guests?"

The doctor, surprised at such a question replied, "What guests are you talking about?"

"Don't you know what I'm talking about?" She asked. "I've prepared a fine dinner for our guests."

Sir Floriano said with greater amazement, "It seems to me that you're delirious today."

His wife said, "I know that I haven't gone out of my mind. You had a big eel sent to me so that I could prepare it because you were bringing some other doctors here for dinner, and I've done what you've sent word for me to do. But if you say this isn't so, we haven't lost anything."

He said, "I don't know what you're talking about. But God sent someone here who did nicely by us, and may he continue to send us what's his without taking what's ours. But certainly this time we were chosen by mistake."

The woman, who had carelessly given away the chalice, realized that her husband truly knew nothing about this, and said with a great and sudden shock, "Sir, to me it seems entirely the opposite since the man who brought the fish also told me that you wanted me to give him the silver chalice that, just a short time before, you had sent with the silversmith's boy. He told me these details so precisely that I gave it to him."

When Sir Floriano heard that the chalice was gone, he quickly realized that someone had tricked them, and he said, "You senseless fool, you've been tricked!"

He quickly left his house and reached the square where he went searching without knowing what he was searching for. He asked everyone he met if they had seen anyone go toward his house with a fish, and he raved about a thousand other things without it bearing any fruit. He went here and there, to the tax office and every other place he could think of. Sometimes, with cold hope, he believed that the chalice had only been taken as a joke.

Andreuccio lingered on the edge of the piazza like an honest person and, though he figured that his companion and the chalice were at safe haven, it still irked him that he spent so much on the eel without having a chance to taste it. So he proposed another deception, no less remarkable than the first, in order to recover the eel. He took the opportunity, while Sir Floriano was so tormented in his search, to hurry to his house. He arrived and with a happy voice he said, "My lady, I bring you good news. Your husband has found the chalice which his companions stole from him as a joke. He has sent me here, however, so I could bring him the fish that you've prepared, since he wants to share it with his friends who played the trick."

The woman, who had been suffering great pain and torment for having been blamed for the loss of the chalice, was very glad to hear that her husband had found it and, quite pleased, she took two great tin platters and put the delicious fish in them, covered them with a fragrant white tablecloth, and gave it all to Andreuccio. Once he was outside the house, he wrapped everything under his cloak and took off to San Michele where he found Liello and the prior, and in good spirits they enjoyed the fine lamprey. They gave the platters to the prior, carefully sold the chalice, and left without any trouble.

Because he couldn't get any information all day about his chalice, Sir Floriano returned late in the evening, hungry and very cross. His wife went to greet him, and she said, "Praise God! You've found the chalice. Even though you called me a fool."

He said to her in his bitter mood, "Get away from me, you depraved lunatic, if you don't want to press your luck, because it seems that besides the damage you caused with your foolishness, you also want to tease me."

The woman, confused by this, timidly said, "Sir, I'm not teasing." And she told him about the second deception she suffered. So much delirium and pain fell on Sir Floriano because of this that he nearly went out of his mind. Many times he tried with subtle and various inquiries to find the deceivers but he never could discover anything about them, and for a long time he lived a miserable life with his wife and continued to be angry with her. So, the Romans enjoyed themselves because they accomplished their tricks and left the doctor with mockery, pain, and loss.

You can't deny that, though the tricksters in this story managed to play both ends, their tricks were full of incredible boldness and danger. And though it's commonly said that the greatest risks bring the most plentiful gains, still those who take these kinds of risks often end up in trouble and, in one stroke, they pay both damages and interest.

HOW VIOLA TRIED TO SATISFY HER THREE LOVERS ON THE SAME NIGHT

Masuccio Salernitano

This past January in Naples there was a good man and woodworker who was a master of nothing but making clogs. This man rented a pigeon coop in the saddler's quarter and kept a larger nest behind the Old Mint. He had a charming and beautiful wife named Viola who, even as a youth, didn't disdain the yearnings of her almost infinite lovers. Still, among the large number of her men, there were those who were more loved and favored than others. One of them was a blacksmith, her neighbor, another was a Genoese merchant, and the third was a monk whose order and habit I don't recall. I do know, however, that this monk was an expert and famous sportsman. Viola promised all three of them, without them knowing anything of the promises made to the others, that when her husband had to stay away from home overnight, she'd satisfy their desires.

After several days, her husband went to Ponte a Selece to retrieve a considerable cargo of mislaid clogs so that he could polish them in Naples, as he usually did, and it required him to stay overnight. All three men looked forward to his departure and made their reservations in advance. Each one placed himself in line, and the first one who presented himself for battle at Viola's door was the Genoese, perhaps the most fervent lover. When he begged her tenderly to expect him to come for dinner and to stay the night, he made greater promises to her than were customary or necessary in such arrangements. Be - cause she didn't want to delay him, Viola said that she'd be delighted, but that he should come late at night so he wouldn't be seen by her neighbors in the quarter. The Genoese most happily replied, "I'll do it, by God!" He left in a hurry and went to the merchants at the loggia, and back and forth to the shops at the Pendino where he bought two oversized capons that were long, white and plump, along with some fresh bread, the best wine, and many other things, and he sent them secretly to the young woman's house.

The monk, after he celebrated the divine office, was looking forward to the promise made to him, and he headed off like a ravenous wolf ready to drag down and devour any lost sheep of the flock. He arrived at Viola's house and called her, saying that he was planning to come to stay the night with her. Viola wouldn't have deceived the Genoese for anything, but knowing that the monk was very reckless and difficult, she knew she wouldn't be able to refuse him. She was so confused, she didn't know what to decide. However, since she was a prudent person, it quickly occurred to her that with proper planning, she could provide for both of them, and so she replied with gracious tones to the monk that she'd agree to his request but that he shouldn't come before five o'clock, because her little brother-in-law would come to stay with her and wouldn't be asleep until then. He could have his desire if he'd go quickly with God. The monk saw that he'd be welcome and didn't care about the rest, so he agreed to this and left.

The blacksmith, who was at the forge until late, busy smelting metal, found Viola at her window when he was going home and said, "Since your husband isn't home tonight, you could welcome me into your good graces, and it would be good if you did. Otherwise you can be sure that your designs on me will be ruined."

Viola who loved him a great deal and was afraid of him, thought that there'd be enough time during the long night to be free for all three patrons. Just as she had found a way for two, so she proposed to include a third, even though he'd be last, and she said to him, "My Mauro, you know how I'm poorly tolerated in this quarter, and how much everyone, with good reason, wants to chase me out. You know how they watch me until midnight. However, so that they can't catch me with their ambush, wait until daybreak, the hour when you always get up, and give me a signal and I'll open the door for you. We'll stay together for a while this first time and then, eventually, we'll make better arrangements."

The smith was satisfied with these arrangements, since he knew that her words were tinged with reason and that he'd have his wish. So he left without saying anything else.

When night came, the Genoese secretly entered Viola's house. Though she happily welcomed him and kissed him many times, nevertheless because he was a little cold, his lustful appetites were not easily aroused without the heat of the bed or other incentives, so she put herself on the horse and began to mix her salad until the capons were plucked and roasted. Then, either because of a bad fire or

for whatever reason, she still went on struggling, worrying that the second dish would turn up before the first
plate was tasted. It was already three o'clock by then, and
their dinner hadn't yet begun when, in the midst of
things, they heard a knock at the door. The Genoese was
quite frightened and said, "It seems to me that someone's
knocked on your door."

The young lady replied, "That's true. I wonder if it's
my brother, but don't be afraid because I'll arrange it so
that he won't see you. Jump out this window and sit
down in that small arbor of herbs there, while I see who it
is and what they want. Then I'll send them away
quickly."

The Genoese was more cold with fright than hot with
passion, and even though outside there was a fierce rain
driven by a very cold wind – which many might have
thought was snow – he still did what Viola said. She
locked him outside and, guessing who was at the door,
she hid the dinner. She went to the door, saw that it was
the bothersome monk, and somewhat agitated she said to
him, "You've come too soon and haven't followed my
instructions. What a mess! Since you couldn't wait a little
while, you've put me in danger of death."

After giving him a piece of her mind, she opened the
door anyway, and he entered without the ceremony of
kisses that the Genoese had made. Swiftly without even
locking the door, he gave her a plenary indulgence that he
bestowed, not with his authority as a cleric, but with his
power as a man. Viola believed that this would be enough
to send him away content until she saw him climbing the
stairs. She locked the door and followed him upstairs

saying, "Go away, for the love of God, since my brother-in-law isn't asleep yet, and he'll hear you for certain."

The monk paid no attention to her but went on up and, finding the fire still warm, he scratched himself a little, joined in battle with Viola again, and began to play a new ballad with an even more delightful melody than the song that the poor Genoese, with his teeth chattering from the cold, had just played. The Genoese saw everything through the slats of the window and was as distressed by his fear of being seen there as by the terrible cold that he endured. Several times he considered jumping off the side of the building but he couldn't determine its height in the darkness. He also hoped that the monk would leave, since the young woman had obviously done her duty by him, and she was continuously urging him to leave.

But the monk was stirred up again by the pleasure of this beautiful young woman, and without letting go of Viola, he taught her many new modern dances, and not only to her, but also to the Genoese who looked on with little pleasure. He decided not to leave until the light of day chased him away.

So he remained for ten hours until he heard the smith who gave the agreed–upon signal and knocked on Viola's door. The monk turned to the young woman and asked, "Who's at the door?"

She replied, "It's the continuous goad of my neighbor, the smith. I haven't been able to get rid of him with a good or a bad reply." It quickly occurred to the monk, who was very witty, to make a joke of this, and swiftly he went down to the door and in a soft voice, as if he were Viola, asked, "Who's there?"

He replied, "It's me. Don't you recognize me? Please open the door and let me come in because I'm getting soaked."

The monk said, "Oh how sad! I can't open the door because it makes too much noise, and scandal will follow."

With no place to escape from the rain, he urged Viola to open up because he was totally consumed with love for her. The monk, who detained him with pleasure to get him soaked, said to him, "My beloved, kiss me through this opening since it's good and wide, while I try quietly to open this damned door."

The smith rose up and happily prepared to kiss her. The monk, in the meantime, dropped his trousers and offered up the opening that he used to discharge his excess bilge. The smith at first believed that he was meeting the sweet lips of Viola but soon could tell by touch and by odor what the opening really was. He guessed that it belonged to another hunter who was more insistent than he and, having taken away his pleasure so nastily, wanted to trick him.

He quickly resolved that this contempt wouldn't go unrewarded and pretending to nibble and lick, he said, "My Viola, I'll go for my cape since I can't endure the rain any longer. In the meantime, try to open this door for me."

The monk replied, "Go in the name of God, and return quickly!" And he laughed with the young woman until they couldn't stand up. The smith went into his shop and quickly made a rod of iron that looked like a spear, and he heated it and said to his shop boy, "Pay attention, and when I spit, be nimble and bring this staff to me."

Then the smith went back again to try to enter Viola's
house and, from one word to the next, he said, "Kiss me
again."

The monk, who was as quick as a monkey, quickly
offered up the same abyss. Mauro gave the signal to his
apprentice, who very quickly presented him with the red
hot iron that he had in his hand. Taking his time, he
jabbed him right up his *vallum unguis* at least a palm's
length. The monk felt the savage blow and let out a
scream that reached the heavens. When they heard him
howling like a wounded bull, all the neighbors woke up,
got their lights, and opened their windows, upset and
curious about the reason for such a tremendous noise.

The sad Genoese was so numb that he, in just a little
while, would've ended his days changed into ice by the
cold rain. He heard the uproar and saw all the lights in the
neighborhood, and since dawn was already near, he didn't
want to be found there and put to shame like a thief. As a
last resort he decided to jump and, taking heart, he rec-
ommended himself to God and leapt. His fortune was so
favorable that when he landed on the ground his foot
found a stone, and he turned it so that he fractured his leg
in several places. He was as overwhelmed by the incredible pain as the monk, and he also let out a great shout
because of the pain.

The smith ran toward the noise and discovered the
Genoese, and saw why he was shouting. He had some
compassion, and with the help of his apprentice they
dragged him, with considerable effort, back to the shop.
They learned from him what had happened, how it had
happened, who the monk was, and how he was put
outside. The smith silenced the neighbors, saying that it

was two of his apprentices who had been injured. Finally when everyone was as quiet as the monk had become, Viola softly called the smith, who entered the house and found the monk half dead. After they discussed the pros and cons, the smith and his servant put the monk on their shoulders and took him up to his monastery. When the smith came back he had the Genoese carried to his room on a donkey. Then he went back to Viola's house – it was morning by now – and together they ate the capons. In addition to that, they satisfied their desires entirely, so that he returned to beat his hammer very contented. And so this master had the last word and left the others with jokes and injury and pain.

Viola will be considered a prudent person and rightly commended for giving on the same night, and in the right spirit, satisfaction to her three admirers. And although two of them went home as they came – all by themselves – Viola stayed behind, with the plenary indulgence that the venerable monk had given to her many times, to teach the smith all the new dances, which the Genoese, who watched them with little pleasure, had already learned.

TWO DEAR FRIENDS

Masuccio Salernitano

🐍

Not very far from our town is a place hardly anyone knows about and even fewer people visit. It is still inhabited by crude rustic people, just as when, not long ago, two young men, one a miller called Agostino, and the other a shoemaker called Petruccio, lived there. They were extraordinary friends and companions since childhood. Each one had a very young and pretty wife, and they were all so close together that they were seldom or never apart.

This perfect love continued, even when the shoemaker, whose wife was quite beautiful, happened to like his friend's wife somewhat more. Perhaps, now and then, he wished to change dishes. One day, when he had more than the usual opportunity to be together with her, he was able to tell her about his desire. So he unveiled his passion to Catarina, as the miller's wife was named. She heard what he wanted and, even though it wasn't terribly unpleasant, she still indignantly sent him off without an answer. As always, she met Salvaggia, the shoemaker's wife, and told her how Petruccio had challenged her to battle. As much as this upset the shoemaker's wife, she listened to Catarina, and though she was quite offended, it occurred to her that she could take revenge on her

husband one day and still not ruin their very long friendship. After she thanked her dear companion, she asked
Catarina to promise Petruccio that one of these nights she
would wait for him in her bed. But instead of Catarina,
Salvaggia would be there, so that they would have a great
laugh. The miller's wife wanted to please Salvaggia and so
she agreed.

A few days later Petruccio found himself with Catarina,
and he repeated his request even more urgently than
before. She wanted to put the plot she and Salvaggia had
concocted into effect, and so after beating around the bush
for a while she appeared to decide on a way they could
meet. The young woman said, "I'm agreeable, and if my
husband is busy at the mill tonight, then come to my
bed."

Petruccio, extremely happy, answered, "I've just come
from the mill, and there's so much grain that the night
will be two-thirds over before it's all fed to the grinding
stones."

She said, "Praised be God's name! Come between two
and three tonight because I'll wait for you and leave the
door open, you know, just as I usually leave it for my
husband. Be absolutely quiet and come to my bed. But
tell me, how will you leave your wife, since I'm more
afraid of her than death?"

He answered, "I've just decided to lie to her and to tell
her that I have to leave town."

She said, "That sounds fine."

When they finished their discussion, Petruccio went to
the mill to reassure himself that his companion was very
busy, while Catarina told her friend of the plans her
husband had made. Petruccio found the miller completely

occupied with his work at the mill and returned to his house. There he pretended to be preoccupied with his business, and he told his wife that he had to leave immediately for Policastro to buy leather for the workshop.

His wife, who knew where he was going said, "So go!" Laughing to herself she said, "This time buy your own leather and not someone else's skin."

Petruccio pretended to leave and hid someplace in town and waited there, biding his time. When it was night, Catarina went to Salvaggia's house, and according to their plot, she stayed there while Salvaggia went to Caterina's house and went to bed, waiting with pleasure for her own husband and the following battle. She repeated to herself what she would say to him afterwards.

When he thought it was time, Petruccio slowly approached his friend's house, and when he was almost ready to enter he heard something, and he knew that the miller was returning to his house. The mill must have broken, he thought, so that he wouldn't be able to do any more work that night. Therefore, frightened and not very happy, Petruccio returned to his house without anyone seeing or hearing him, and he said to himself, "There'll be another time for what I wanted now."

But so that the night didn't become a total loss, he started to knock slowly but hard and to call his wife to open the door. Catarina, who knew his voice, not only didn't open the door, but she didn't even answer him, staying quiet so he wouldn't discover the trick. He was somewhat upset about this and exhausted himself trying to open his door. When he finally got in, he went straight to bed and embraced the woman who pretended to be sleeping so soundly. He woke her up and, since he believed that she was his wife, he made up excuses, inventing a story about why he hadn't gone away. Then he undressed himself and laid on his side. Since he was already prepared for battle he decided that, since he couldn't plow his neighbor's land, he would sow his seeds in his own field. Because he believed that she was Salvaggia, he gave a good thrashing to Catarina who was locked in his embrace. The poor woman endured this with pleasure and patience to make him believe that she was his wife.

Meanwhile, the miller went wearily into his own house and went to sleep in his bed. He lay still without making any noise. Salvaggia believed that he was her husband and she happily welcomed him without a word. After she waited a little while, she sensed that her lover didn't want to do battle, and so she gave him a heartier welcome so that she herself wouldn't be the person who was deceived and mocked in the enterprise. The miller believed that he was with his own wife, and even though he needed sleep more than a skirmish, when he felt the nibbles and scratches, he was forced to his job, and he poured water once from on top, but not to his mill.

Then it finally seemed time to Salvaggia to let on that the game was up, and she broke her silence and said, "Oh you traitor! You disloyal dog. You thought you had your dear friend's wife in your arms. You thought you were busy elsewhere, helping yourself to what is your friend's, and you've shown more energy than you usually do, proving that you're very hardy, although at home you seem worn out. But God have mercy, this time your plans have failed. Don't worry, I won't forget this."

She attacked him like this and even worse, nagging him so that he'd respond. But the poor miller was mute, although he understood what she said. Not only did he understand that she was his dear friend's wife, but, in fact, he even understood how his predicament came to pass, so that his pleasure was quickly converted into sheer horror. Yet he continued to keep silent and got out of bed, and although morning still hadn't dawned, he quickly went to where he realized his wife must be, and he called his friend who came outside full of suspicion. Agostino said, "My brother, because of you both of us have been hurt and shamed, but it's more discrete to be silent than to speak, and there's no need for us to quarrel about it."

With great regret he told in detail how everything had happened, adding that to him it seemed that even if Fortune had favored the cleverness and maliciousness of their wives, they wouldn't want to be enemies or ruin their long friendship. He added that what had happened by deception would have happened by nature. Since in the past all of them had gotten along so well together, they decided to share their wives and stay together in the future with all four of them happy and satisfied. In this way they would amend the regrettable error of the past.

Petruccio heard the solution of his dear friend, who had taken delight in the woman he himself loved, and saw that the affair had ended in love and good will, so he decided to try even harder to keep his friend. He knew that, because of his shortcomings, his friend ought to have rejected him rather than lose the world's honor, which, as you can clearly see today, is not worth much when it's not sold or bartered for the most vile things. He agreed that he'd be happy, since the result would be convenient, peaceful and quiet, to do as the miller proposed. And to conclude this agreement among them all, they called Catarina, since she wasn't deceived, and they decided to call Salvaggia right away. When they all gathered to-gether and revealed how the trick had gone wrong, and, considered their marriages and their friendships, they decided to establish a union of peace and quiet among them. And so, from then on, there were no divisions among them, neither of wives nor of anything else. In the end their children thought of both women as their mothers.

There will be some who'll scorn the agreement that I've described to you of the two dear friends who put their friendship before their honor. But I doubt that those people understand that if other things in the heavens don't change, this honor, which today only the virtuous value and celebrate, will come to an end, since it will be, with general contempt, not only disapproved of, but exiled forever to the ends of the earth.

A TRICK PLAYED BY THE SCHEGGIA
ON NERI CHIARAMONTESI

Antonfrancesco Grazzini

🎋

At the time of the Scheggia, Monaco, and Pilucca, three men who were great partners and friends as well as witty and clever masters of tricks, there lived in Florence a certain Neri Chiaramontesi, a noble and well-to-do man, but as uncorked and shrewd as any man in our city. There was never anyone who took more delight than he did in joking and jousting with others. Most of the time he found himself with these three companions having dinner in the house of Sir Mario Tournaquinci, who was known as the Knight of the Golden Spurs, a very rich and honorable man. In his day Neri had played thousands of jokes and hoaxes on them but they were never able to come up with a way to avenge themselves. This particularly bothered the Scheggia, who always brooded over it.

And so, along with the others, he found himself again one evening in the parlor room of this knight sitting around a good fire talking, since it was during the heart of winter, and they had a lot to discuss among them. Neri said to the Scheggia, "Here, now, take this gold coin and go to the Bolognese pilgrim's house – who was in those days a famous courtesan – dressed just as you are, but with paint or ink or something on your hands and face

166

and give her this pair of boots without saying anything to her."

The Scheggia said, "Here's a pair of coins for you if you get all dressed up in white armor with a sickle on your shoulder and go up to the merchant Ceccherino's shop." At that time this place was on the corner of Vacchereccia where almost all the best and most wealthy young men of Florence gathered.

"Okay!" Neri replied laughing. "But you must give me the coins."

"I will," said the Scheggia. "But listen. I want you to show the people there that you're enraged by making a commotion and threatening to cut them all to pieces."

"Leave it to me," said Neri. "But I haven't seen the money yet." Then the Scheggia took two new coins from his purse and said, "Here they are as a pledge to the knight. If you do your work, they'll be yours."

Neri agreed, thinking that by taking from the Scheggia's hand those two florins, which he held dearer than any other ten, he'd be able to mock him and cheat him. He quickly began to select his armor from among the many suits in the house of the knight, who could out-fit a hundred men, since he was a great friend of the older Lorenzo de' Medici who ruled Florence. Neri put on his armor while the Scheggia called Monaco and Pilucca aside. He told them what he wanted them to do, then sent them on their way. He stayed behind and chatted with the knight while watching this man don the armor. He was armed and ready to go precisely at two o'clock. Finally, Neri fastened his headpiece and put the sickle over his shoulder and set off toward the corner shop of Ceccherino. But he marched very slowly because of the weight of the armor and the shin guards. The shin guards, which were a bit long, made it difficult for him to raise and move his feet.

Meanwhile, Monaco and Pilucca had gone out to do their duty. One went to the merchant's shop and the other up to the school of the old Greek who had taught them to fence in the tower near the Old Market. In front of a number of people Monaco and Pilucca swore that Neri Chiaramontesi was out of his mind – as the Scheggia had arranged – and that he wanted to kill his mother back at his house and throw all of their things down a well. They described how at Sir Tournaquinci's house he had dressed up in a suit of white armor, then took a sickle in his hand and made everyone flee. Pilucca, who had gone to the fencing school, said that Neri had, in the end, said that he wanted to go to the shop to beat Ceccherino senseless.

Most of those Florentine people set off to see the entertainment, since they didn't much like the merchant who was an arrogant, presumptuous, ignorant and worthless person. He had a slanderous tongue, the most treacherous in Florence. So huge an eater and a flatterer, I can't describe it. Nevertheless, with all that, he always had a shop full of noble and honorable young men. Monaco also told them about Neri's unbelievable madnesses. In the meantime Neri had left the knight's house and passed Santa Maria Novella, and everyone who saw him looked on astonished and grinning. Finally he reached Ceccherino's shop and, as soon as he arrived, he shoved the door with all his might and burst it open.

Encased in the armor Neri came in menacingly shouting, "All right, traitors, you're dead," and he hoisted the sickle. His abrupt arrival, his armor, his shouting and his sickle raised in the air, terrified everyone. In fact, some fled into the draper's shop, some hid in the showroom, some took shelter under the benches, and under the tables, some screamed, some cursed, some shrieked, and some begged for God's mercy. The greatest turmoil in the world ensued.

The Scheggia, who had followed closely behind Neri, knew immediately that he was near Ceccherino's shop, and he took off running, flying into Portarossa, where Neri's uncle, Agnolo Chiaramontesi, an old man and re - sponsible citizen of good reputation, worked at the Wool Guild. He told Agnolo that he should run to Ceccherino's shop so that Neri, who had lost his senses and gone mad dressed all in armor with a sickle in hand, wouldn't do any great damage. Agnolo, who didn't have any children, replied, "Oh my, what are you telling me?"

"The truth," said the Scheggia, and he added, "Hurry, come at once, but call four or six of those people who are your box packers so they can hold down him, tie him up and then, once he's restrained, lead him home. After three or four days in the dark there, without letting anyone speak to him, he'll quickly return to his senses."

That man, who didn't consider himself a person easily tricked, believed everything the Scheggia said. Quickly he called six of the youngest and strongest men from among the wool beaters, and with two sets of ropes they went away in a flash to Ceccherino's shop not far away. There they found Neri, who had endangered all these people. They were still terrorized that he might actually strike someone. Neri, who was really enjoying himself, swung his sickle so that even Bevilacqua would have been taken aback. He turned round and round, but always careful to strike where he could cause the greatest fear and the least harm.

When his uncle arrived and recognized his voice, he hurled himself on Neri, and grabbed the sickle and shouted, "Get hold of yourself. What are you doing, nephew?" And he turned to those men he had brought with him and said, "Come on! You, take off his armor. Pin him to the ground and tie him up quickly." Those men immediately threw themselves on him. Some took him by the legs, some by the arms, and some by the neck until they stretched him out on the pavement, giving him the opportunity to exhaust himself and not allowing him to catch his breath. Shouting in a loud voice he said, "What are you doing, traitors, I'm not mad." He could only pant since they had tied his arms and legs up so that he wasn't even able to squirm. Someone found a ladder and tied him firmly on it so that he wouldn't throw himself on the ground. The Scheggia, who was standing at the side, heard how he whined, threatened, and cursed, and he felt such joy that he was beside himself. The people who had fled and hid, heard and saw that the madman was tied up, and they came from their hiding places. They looked at him carefully, and he told them all that he was sorry, showing it clearly with both gestures and words.

You can imagine, then, how Neri, who was by nature supremely arrogant and eccentric, wore himself out with worry. He never stopped shouting or menacing, unaware that he was making his situation worse. Agnolo had his workers lift the ladder. He flung his cloak on top and made them carry Neri home, where Monaco had arrived to tell Neri's mother everything that had happened. She and the uncle arranged to put him in the master bedroom on the bed, tied just as he was, and they were determined not to say anything to him and not to give him anything until morning and then, once they had called the doctors, they'd take care of him as they saw fit. On the advice of the Scheggia everyone decided to return to what they were doing.

In the meantime, this story spread throughout Florence, and the Scheggia went off happily with his companions to find the knight. They told him blow by blow of their great success. He was in a cheerful and joyous mood, and, because it was already four o'clock, they stayed to dine with him without having Neri around to drive them crazy.

So Neri was left alone in the dark, tied up in bed as if he were mad. He understood his trouble. With only his helmet and the shin guard removed, and otherwise covered quite well, he stayed quiet for a good while. He thought over what had happened again and again, and he was certain that it was the work of the Scheggia that brought him to this end, with his uncle, his mother, and all of Florence thinking he was a madman. Therefore, he felt so much pain and regret that if he had been free he would've done some great harm either to himself or to someone else. He stayed like this, enraged and sleepless, until midnight when he was assaulted by hunger and thirst. He shouted as loud as he could, and he continuously called his mother and then the servant to bring him something to eat and drink. But you can be sure that they pretended not to hear him.

At about two o'clock in the morning his uncle arrived with his cousin, a friar of San Marco, and with two physicians, the best in the city at that time. While his mother held a light, they opened the door and found Neri where they had left him that evening. He was in discomfort from shouting so much, and he was hungry and thirsty from not having had anything to eat or drink, and he was tired from lack of sleep, so that he was now so weakened that he was as meek as a little lamb. When those people arrived, Neri lifted his head and greeted them kindly and then begged them to listen to him say just a hundred words without any interruption, and to hear his explanation. Agnolo and the others courteously said that he could say what he liked, and he began to speak. Starting from the beginning he told the entire story in order, point by point, explaining how the Scheggia had betrayed him and had him held and tied up like a madman. And then he added, "If you want to make this absolutely clear to yourselves, go to the house of Sir Tournaquinci, our neighbor, and you'll see that he still has the two gold coins in deposit."

When they heard him speak so sensibly and explain his reasons so well, his uncle and the physicians thought that he was telling them the truth, since they knew very well who the Scheggia was. So, Agnolo, the friar and one of the physicians went to the knight, and they discovered that all that Neri had told them was true. Moreover, Sir Mario told them that the Scheggia and his comrades had dined that evening with him and that they had had the best laugh in the world. So they returned to Neri immediately, and his uncle was quite ashamed. He untied Neri with his own hands, took off his armor and asked his forgiveness. Fired up with indignation and the greatest rage he heaped abuse on the Scheggia. Neri, nearly out of his mind, decided to light a big fire at once. He thanked them all and said "good-night," and had the servants bring him something to eat. And as soon as he had a good meal, he climbed into bed to get the rest he needed.

The story was already known throughout all of Florence from the mouths of the three companions and the physicians, and it was known in all its detail. It even reached the ears of the Magnificent, who sent for the Scheggia so that he could tell him every word. When Neri heard this he was so desperate that he was tempted to give them – and the Scheggia especially – a beating to avenge himself. But since he had played many tricks on them and on others, he figured that too much shame and perhaps too much harm might result from it, so he decided on another course of action. Without letting another living person know except his mother, he went to Rome and then to Naples where he signed on as second mate on a ship. In due time he became master of this ship, but he never returned to Florence until he was so old that the matter had been forgotten. The Scheggia and his companions devoted themselves to having a good time, delighted above all that they had gotten rid of the sight of that man.

A Trick Played by the Scheggia on Gian Simone Berrettaio

Antonfrancesco Grazzini

The Scheggia and Pilucca, as you may have heard, were astute and witty companions, and men who liked to have a good time, and they were reasonable masters of their respective arts, the one being a goldsmith and the other a sculptor. And although they were rather poor, they were cordial enemies of hard work and lived cheerfully, having the best time in the world and without any worldly care. By chance they became friends with a certain Gian Simone, a hat-maker without much talent, but well-off. He had a shop on the corner of Via de' Pecori, and men gathered in his little storefront, especially in the winter. The Scheggia and Pilucca often came to pass the time, sometimes playing cards at a table there alone, other times playing tarots, and besides talking they often drank from a flask. Because the Scheggia was an accomplished speaker and troubadour of the most beautiful stories, he often told tales about ghosts and enchantments that de-lighted and fascinated his audience.

Around this time, Gian Simone was captivated by his neighbor, a widow who was beautiful beyond measure, but since she was noble and decent and suitably blessed by the goods of Fortune, he was distressed about this. He didn't know where his love for her would lead and he didn't have a ready cure for it, so he thought he would pluck the fruit of his desire by the powers of enchantment. One day he called on the Scheggia, since he had the greatest faith in him. He told him about his desire and sought his advice after first making him swear that he wouldn't tell anyone. The Scheggia obligingly said that he'd do everything he could, but he needed to discuss it with Pilucca, because Pilucca had a friend called Zoroastro, a person who could make the demons do whatever he wished.

Gian Simone said that he was delighted to hear about this, so they decided to dine together the following evening at Gian Simone's house to discuss and decide what to do about the question of his love. Elated, the Scheggia went to find Pilucca as soon as he left Gian Simone, and he told him everything that Gian Simone had said, point by point. Together they had a great laugh, because besides the fun they would have with this, they planned to extract some profit. They decided what they had to do, and each one went about his business.

The next evening, All Saints Day, they arrived at an early hour at Gian Simone's shop. After a little while he brought them home to his house where he had arranged for a splendid dinner. Once they had eaten some fruit Gian Simone sent the women to their room, and the men started to discuss Gian Simone and his love. The Scheggia asked Pilucca if he'd ask Zoroastro to cast a spell, as he had already done for countless other men, so that Gian Simone could enjoy his beloved and possess her. Pilucca said he'd make every effort and would come back the

next day with his answer, thinking that at least he'd surely hear some good stories from him, and finally they left.

Gian Simone felt relieved and glad, but it seemed that it
would be a thousand years before he'd find himself with
his widow. The two companions made various proposals
before they went to bed. The next morning they went to
find their friend Zoroastro to tell him their plan. He liked
it a lot, and recalled similar intrigues, and he was anxious
to go ahead with it. He suggested several things to them
and together they found different ways to draw Gian
Simone into the plot and leave him hanging. They decided that Pilucca would go and find Gian Simone and
tell him that the necromancer had agreed to do what he
wanted but he would have to pay twenty-five florins in
advance. After they left Zoroastro, Pilucca went to Gian
Simone's shop to tell him everything. It seemed very
strange to Gian Simone that he would have to pay
twenty-five florins in advance. But he didn't want to
make a decision at that exact moment, so he told Pilucca
that he'd meet the Scheggia for dinner and then make up
his mind. He said that he didn't want to do anything
without his advice.

Pilucca liked this idea and went to meet the Scheggia,
who was waiting for him in Santa Reparata. He told him
everything that they had said, and the Scheggia was
pleased. They took a long walk until it was time for
dinner and then they went to dine at Gian Simone's
house, which was on Via Fiesolana. He came to the door
to meet them, took them by the hands and led them
inside to dine. After they were brought their food they
discussed the enchantment and the enchanter for a while,
as well as the fact that Gian Simone didn't want to pay

those twenty-five florins, much less pay them in advance. Still, when they explained to him that the necromancer would arrange it so that his lady wouldn't be able to live without him, the Scheggia made Gian Simone agree to the proposition. Before paying the money, however, Gian Simone wanted to see proof of the necromancer's art so that he could be confident that he might find himself with his beloved. "You know very well," said the Scheggia, "that he's an honest man and he'll make you see things that will amaze you and assure you of everything. But have you given any thought to how you'd like to enjoy your first time with her? Tell me."

"Not yet," replied Gian Simone.

Pilucca said, "I think it would be best if you had him make her come the first time to your bed naked at midnight and then he could make her fall in love with you from then on, so that she wouldn't want any god but you, and like salt in water, she'd be consumed and melted by your lovemaking. And he can make her come after you with more fervor than a sheep to salted bread."

"You know what I want," said Gian Simone. "You couldn't think of a better way for him to do it. But before I count the money I intend to see some proof, not because I don't have faith in you and in him but just so I don't seem like a person at his wit's end. I'd rather show that I'm a man not a shadow. I want to proceed with every-thing properly proven, so the enchanter will take me much more seriously."

"He can't blame you for that," said the Scheggia, "Well spoken! So, the evening after next, that's Sunday, we'll go together to his house in Gualfonda and you'll see some of his miracles. They discussed many other things,

Antonfrancesco Grazzini

and planning to meet again on Sunday evening in Santa Maria Novella, they left. Gian Simone happily went to his shop while his two companions went to find Zoroastro, who was a man about thirty-six or forty years old. He was large with an olive complexion, and he had a forbidding and fierce expression and an untidy black beard that hung down on his chest. He was very freakish and strange to look at.

Zoroastro devoted himself to alchemy, and he had gone deeply inside the darkness of his incantations. He had seals, letters, amulets, pentacles, bells, stoves and furnaces of various sorts to distill herbs, soil, metals, stones, and woods. He also had parchment made from the skin of an unborn calf, the eyes of lynx, drool from a mad dog, spines of pigeon fish, bones of the dead, nooses from the hanged, daggers and swords that had murdered men, the clavicle and the knife of Salome, and herbs and seeds gathered at various phases of the moon and under various constellations, along with thousands of tales and gossip to put fear into fools.

He devoted himself to astrology, to physiognomy, to chiromancy and to a hundred other strange sciences. He believed in witches, but above all, he followed spirits. But despite all that, he had never been able to accomplish a thing outside the laws of nature, although he could tell about thousands of blunders and mistakes, and he'd make you believe that he could produce results in people. Because he had neither father nor mother, and was very well-off, he spent most of his time alone in his house, because he couldn't find a maid or a servant who wasn't afraid to stay with him. He was quite pleased about this and chose to associate little with people. He went around his house with his beard all tangled, never bothering to comb it, and he was always foul and filthy. The common folk believed he was a great philosopher and necromancer.

The Scheggia and Pilucca were his close friends, and they knew to within two hairs how his mind worked and how many days it was until the day of San Biagio. They found him at home and told him about the meeting that took place with Gian Simone, including the discussion of the twenty-five florins, which he'd have to pay in advance. They told him how Gian Simone first wanted some proof to reassure himself that the proposed enchantment would succeed. They told him, in the end, how they had decided to go about providing that proof. Zoroastro was very astute, and he had a number of ways to show Gian Simone proof and then to take advantage of his love for the widow, and they all agreed about the endless little details and decided what they had to do. Zoroastro told them that he'd wait for them on Sunday evening there in his house where everything would be ready.

The two men left very merry because they'd be able to spend money for many days and weeks at the expense of Gian Simone. They passed the interim engaged in various amusements and other vagrancies. In the meanwhile, Gian Simone saw his widow every morning, fat and fresh, and he pined away and was consumed like snow in the sun. It seemed that it would be thousands of years before he could draw her close to him, often saying to himself, "Ah, traitor! Patarine bitch! You haven't once looked straight at me. Maybe I've fallen in love with you, but there will come a time when I'll make you weep with burning eyes! Leave it to me. If I get my claws into you, by the body of the Antichrist, you'll understand what I'm saying." Often when he saw either the Scheggia or Pilucca, he did nothing but beg them and remind them of what they had promised.

Sunday finally came, and Gian Simone had no sooner finished eating than he went to Santa Maria Novella to hear vespers, then compline, and lauds. Just as he was leaving, since it was already almost time for the Ave Maria, he met the two companions. He said "good evening," and greeted them by saying, "I had begun to worry. You're so late."

"It's not late, no," replied the Pilucca. "We agreed to go there on the half hour." In a little while they brought him to Zoroastro's house, just as it began to get dark. They knocked on the door twice to make the situation more dramatic, and Zoroastro came to the top of the stairs with a candlestick in his hand to give them some light. They climbed the stairs and arrived in the hall, where he received them with a cheerful grin and asked them to sit down. While they were talking, they started to discuss demons and spirits until finally Pilucca turned the conversation round again and said to Zoroastro, "This is that good man I mentioned to you who has fallen in love. He has come to see a sign of your power so that he can be sure you can accomplish what he desires."

Zoroastro turned his frightening eyes toward Gian Simone and looked at him in such a fierce way that he made him shake all over. He said to him, "At the present time I'm prepared to do what you wish, out of love for you, and I don't know if others besides you could get me to do this. But you're my very dear friends and I can not and must not refuse you anything that I can do." He left them there saying he'd return later, and he went into his chamber to dress in a long white gown that reached down to the floor, and he tied a red cord around his waist. On his head he placed a headpiece encircled with imitation serpents that looked all too real. In his left hand he held a vessel made of marble and in his right hand a sponge tied to the shin-bone of a dead man. Dressed like this, he went back into the room. His return brought as much cheer and gladness to the Scheggia and Pilucca as fear and pain to Gian Simone who rather regretted having come.

Zoroastro laid the sponge and vessel on the ground and told the men they shouldn't doubt whatever they heard or saw, nor should they ever mention either God or the saints. When he was all set, he took a little book from his breast pocket and mumbled slowly and quietly as he pretended to read great and profound things. He knelt down and kissed the ground from time to time, and sometimes he gazed up at the sky. He put on the strangest show in the world for a quarter of an hour. Once he was finished with this part of his operation, he opened the vessel, which was full of the tincture of brazil wood, and he plunged the sponge inside saying a little louder, "With this blood of the dragon I make the circle of Pluto." Then he made such a large circle that he took up two-thirds of the room, and he knelt in the middle of it and kissed the ground three times. He asked them to tell him what proof they wanted. Pilucca turned toward Gian Simone, who was trembling like a leaf, and asked him what proof he'd like to see most. Gian Simone turned to the Scheggia and said that he'd let them decide. They came up with many signs, but they didn't like any of them because some were too insignificant, some too profound, some were dangerous, some blasphemous, and no one could come to a decision. Zoroastro, almost laughing, said, "I've decided to make you see a pleasing thing, one that will make you laugh but will nevertheless be of some value. I see the monk, a friend of ours, who's now at the corner of the Old Market, and he's still in his slippers and dressed in a cloak and hood. I want, by the force and virtue of my art, to make him appear here immediately inside this circle." The Scheggia and Pilucca praised this idea, and Gian Simone liked it too. He said that he thought it was a good idea precisely because the monk was his friend.

The monk was a sensual man who was registered with the Silk Guild, but he was devoted to more than this. He had many friends, he leased houses, and was generous in his giving to both man and woman alike, but he'd also do a little scrounging, according to his needs. He was a cheerful person, a balladeer, and very fine harp player. I know enough about him to tell you that he was a naughty man from the forest to the coast, as well as the greatest friend of Zoroastro, the Scheggia and Pilucca. When he heard what his friends were planning for Gian Simone he agreed to help them, and they planned that he'd come to Zoroastro's house that evening, just as you've heard, with two heads of lettuce strung together and a bunch of roots. When they had knocked on the door and came in, he had climbed out onto the edge of the window facing the road. Although he was very uncomfortable, he stood there trying not to fall. Zoroastro adjusted the window and arranged the latch so that the window seemed to be locked, but it wasn't. Even a little push would have opened it. The monk then waited, watching and listening to what went on in the room through a little hole made expressly for him. He waited for his entrance with great joy.

Zoroastro began to speak again, and he said, "Now it's time for me to make it clear to you," and he added, "Our monk has approached a salad-seller. Look at what he's buying, eh, wait a bit," he said, "He has two heads of lettuce and a bunch of roots, oh, oh, now the vendor is stringing them together. Now he's paying but he's giving him more than enough coins, since the salad and roots amount to only six coins." After he said this, he stayed on the ground lying face down. He said some gibberish then stood up and fell down twice. He went across the circle on his knees, and staring intently at the vessel as before he said, "Our monk just received his change and is taking his salad greens toward Via Pellicceria to go home. But in this instant I've raised him invisibly from the earth using demons. Oh, there he is already above the bishop's palace! Oh, he's coming! He's already above the square of Our Lady. Oh, now he's over the *grand dame* Santa Maria Novella, and now he's entered Gualfonda. Oh, there he is in the middle of the street. He's already close by, less than fifty feet away. Oh, there he is right at the window! Now he'll enter the circle wearing his slippers, mantle and hood, carrying his salad greens and roots in hand." Immediately the monk let out a very loud scream, and he began to shout as loud as he could.

When Gian Simone saw this he was so amazed and terrified at the same time that he was nearly struck dead. He wanted to speak but he couldn't summon the words, and because of his extraordinary fear, his body reacted in such a way that he completely filled his pants. The

Scheggia kept saying to him, "What do you say Gian Simone? Isn't this a very clear sign that he can do whatever he wants with evil spirits?"

The monk was shouting in a loud voice, "You traitors, what's going on? Is this how you treat a good man?" While Pilucca tried to comfort the monk, the Scheggia and Zoroastro stood near Gian Simone and noticed that he couldn't speak and his face had turned the color of ashes. They were very worried about him. They grabbed him under his arms, since he was about to sit down, and they began to walk him around the room. But he recovered his spirit a bit and began to say in a trembling voice, "Let's go, let's get out of here. It seems to me thousands of years since I was last at home." He was shaking, and his teeth were chattering so hard he would still feel it many weeks later. The Scheggia took him by the hand without saying a word and started for the top of the stairs, but he hadn't yet taken two steps before he realized, since Gian Simone was still dripping, that the hatter had filled his pants. So he turned to him and said, "Gian Simone, I must tell you that you're pants are full of shit."

"Even Cimabue – who was born blind – would know that," said Pilucca. "Don't you smell how he stinks?"

Gian Simone said, "I'm amazed myself that I didn't shit on my soul, not to mention my heart! I seem to have lost my wits."

"Nevertheless, it would do you good to go someplace and change," said Zoroastro, "so your drippings won't make my house stink. And then, in time, we will see each other again."

So the Scheggia went with him, leaving the monk, who was still complaining, with Pilucca by his side pretending to pacify him. Gian Simone left the house but he didn't want to discuss the matter any further, yet on the entire way back he did nothing but whine and complain about it. Finally, the Scheggia opened the door for him, locked him inside, and then went back to Zoroastro's house to be with his companions who laughed and ate there all night before each one went home.

Once Gian Simone was home he called his wife and his maid from the ground floor, saying that they should hurry and put water on the fire, since he needed to wash himself. His wife, smelling the stench and seeing his face so sad and white asked, "Dear husband, what's happened to you? You seem as if you've been disinterred! What do you have to say?"

Gian Simone said, "My body was in the throes of such sharp pain, which came upon me so quickly and with such a furious impact, that I was ready to die. Hurrying home made the pain even worse but since I didn't have any recourse, I was forced to let it go into my pants."

His wife, who was very feminine, pulled him out of his clothes and with the maid's help they washed him care-fully and put him to bed, as he wanted, without any supper. All night long he lamented, never closing his eyes, and by the beginning of the next day he began to feel a chill and he caught a good fever.

The Scheggia got himself out of bed early that morning and found Pilucca, and at three o'clock they went to Gian Simone's shop where they heard that he was very ill. The Scheggia felt some remorse over this and since he was on familiar terms with Gian Simone, he went to visit him and found him in bed in such a state that he seemed dead. So the Scheggia told him that he wanted to call the doctor because he needed to be treated so that the affair wouldn't be talked about all over Florence.

"Whom will you find?" asked Gian Simone.

The Scheggia replied, "Maestro Samuello Ebreo," who in those times was the best physician in all of Italy.

He left right away so that there would be no delay. He found the physician, who was his very dear friend, and told him the entire story of Gian Simone's illness from beginning to end. The doctor listened with a big smile and readily went with the Scheggia to see this patient, from whom he drew eight or ten ounces of the most tormented and curdled blood that he had ever seen. He said to him, "Gian Simone, don't worry. You are cured." And to make it brief, he made him live a careful and clean life, and in eight or ten days he got out of bed, cured in one stroke of both his fever and his love.

One day the Scheggia went to see Gian Simone, who still hadn't left his house. It seemed a pity to the Scheggia to lose those twenty-five florins. While they were talking, they started to discuss his love and the Scheggia said to him, "Oh, Gian Simone, now that you're cured, by the grace of God, and you've seen some proof, you can easily believe in Zoroastro who's only waiting for the coins to do whatever you want. You can finish this work whenever you're ready and hold your beloved little widow naked in your arms. By the Holy Evangelists, she'd be a delight for someone bold and carefree."

Gian Simone shook his head and said, "You foul man. I'm thankful to you and the necromancer even more. To put it succinctly, I don't want to meddle with demons or spirits. I still tremble when I remember the monk who appeared carried through the air half dead, and you couldn't see who carried him. I swear to you upon my faith that it has made all love of the flesh leave me, and I don't care about the widow anymore. Instead, when I think of her it sickens me, considering that she was almost the reason for my death. Oh, what a fright I had for a while! My hair curls when I think of it, so consequently, I thank Zoroastro, but I won't need his services."

The Scheggia listened to what he had to say, and it seemed to him that this man had become wee tiny, and it also seemed to him that he hadn't accomplished anything, and he said to himself, 'You see, it's not going as well as we all had thought.' And feeling that Gian Simone had scorned him, he answered, "Oh, Gian Simone, what are you saying? You see the necromancer doesn't waste his time worrying. What the devil do you think? What will you do? You're looking for the Virgin Mary in Ravenna. I'm very worried that when Zoroastro hears this from you, he'll lose his temper and think he's been cheated, and then he'll play some strange trick on you. A fine thing, and from upstanding men. Words fail me! Why did you make him show you proof if you were going to decide in the end not to go through with it? He's not one to anger easily, Gian Simone, and that's the truth. But if he turns you into some foul animal it serves you right!"

That man's face had already become like a wet rag with fear. He answered the Scheggia by saying, "'Upon the blood of all the martyrs – which was the oath of the Assassin – tomorrow morning, first thing, I'll go to the Council of Eight and recount the case, and then I'll be noble and praiseworthy. I don't know what keeps me from going now."

As soon as the Scheggia heard mention of the Council his face changed six shades of red and he said to himself, "This isn't the time to beat one's breast. We'll arrange it so that the devil will not be led in procession." He turned to Gian Simone again and began to speak sweetly and said, "Now, Gian Simone, you've gone beyond the limit, and for your sake I wouldn't want, for a thousand florins of gold, for Zoroastro to know what you've said. Oh, don't you know that the Council of Eight has power over men but not over demons? Zoroastro has thousands of ways to make trouble for you that you could never imagine. I think, because he's kind, polite, and generous that you ought to give him a present, without too much expense, of four pair of geese, eight pairs of fat pigeons, ten flasks of some good wine that the Giugni or the Macinghi families sell, six goat cheeses, and sixty prickly pears, and you should send these to him by two litter carriers. He'll consider you more dear and love you more for this, your loving-kindness and liberality, than for a hundred florins. This way you'll have him as your friend. To do otherwise would be worthless, and you'd rap your own knuckles."

Gian Simone liked this very much and said, "I want you to be the one who presents these things on my behalf, and asks pardon for me since you know the whole story and, with my endless thanks, recommend me to him."

"I'd be delighted," replied the Scheggia, "And I'm sure I'll leave him satisfied, and your friend."

"I dearly hope that he'll be satisfied," added Gian Simone, "But his friendship is something I don't care about at all."

Then he calculated how much money these goods would cost, and he gave the Scheggia the money. So the

Scheggia went off to the Old Market and there he hired two basket-carriers. One he sent to buy the wine, the other he sent to the poultry dealer to buy some fat and pretty capons and the pigeons. As soon as the basket-carrier returned with the wine they bought the fruit and then they went back to Gian Simone's house. The Scheggia called Gian Simone to come look out his window, and he said, "I'll go with them."

"Go," said Gian Simone, "Since God wishes you to do good work."

So the Scheggia left with the basket-carriers following behind, and he went to Zoroastro's house. Laughing, he told him about all the discussions between him and Gian Simone. Zoroastro asked the basket-carriers to put down their baskets and unload their wares. He ordered the birds plucked and prepared for the evening meal and refused to leave the house, preferring to stay and watch the basket-carriers work, so that the meal wouldn't go up in smoke.

But the Scheggia went to look for the monk and Pilucca. When he finally found them, he told them the story. They were left very happy with what he told them, but it seemed very sad, nevertheless, to exchange twenty-five florins for a stingy little meal. Pilucca, most of all, wouldn't have agreed to any of the conditions if he had not heard Gian Simone mention the Council of Eight. In the end, they would come to Zoroastro's house that evening and dine together at someone else's expense. The Scheggia left them and went to look for Gian Simone, and on Zoroastro's behalf he gave him a thousands thanks and a thousand prayers. He then returned to Zoroastro's house to stay around to prepare the roasts and make sure that they were cooked to his taste, since he was more devoted to gluttony than Saint Francis was to the girdle. At the specified time, Pilucca and the monk arrived and they had a party together and with many laughs about Gian Simone's affairs, they finally sat down at the table. The basket-carriers and a servant of Zoroastro served them with well-arranged and well-seasoned food, as you might guess. They were fine companions, like a small group of priests with good wine that soothed them.

But then, when they got to the point that they were enjoying the conversations more than the food, Pilucca, the one who held those twenty-five florins close to his heart, couldn't accept their loss, and all of a sudden he began to say, "By God, these capons and pigeons have been tasty and delicate and I don't think that I've ever eaten better cheese nor tasted more precious wine."

Zoroastro replied, "I've arranged to set aside half of everything for tomorrow evening, so that we can dine again just as well as we did this evening. And if you were more patient, I would have invited you, without a doubt."

"I was pretty sure of that," said Pilucca, "But I didn't say it for that reason, but when I eat at someone else's expense, I always like to have more than double. Therefore, I'd like for us to arrange some twist, some snare, some way we can cast a net upon Gian Simone and get those twenty-five florins from him. Just think about how many dinners like this we could make with twenty-five florins. I know you'd say that I would become a pig that weighs more than 600 pounds."

"Come on," said the monk.

"And what would you suggest we do to him?" asked the Scheggia. And so in a few hours Zoroastro and the others came up with several ways to get the money from him. They agreed on the one invented by Pilucca since it was attainable and less dangerous. As soon as they heard about it, they all happily went along with it. Agreed, finally, on what they had to do, they left Zoroastro and went off to get some sleep.

To begin the selected plan, early in the morning, Pilucca wrote a counterfeit summons and took a laborer from the works of Santa Maria del Fiore, where he was a master. This man had just returned from Rome, and he had a short beard that was so blackened by smoke that he looked like an inquisitor. He attached a broadsword to the man's side and sent him to Gian Simone's house, advising and instructing him on what to do and say. The laborer knocked on the door, was led inside, and went to the bedroom guided by the maid. He gave the summons he carried in his hand to Gian Simone, who asked him where he had come from. He answered by saying, "Read this and you'll see!" And so, without saying another word, he began to fidget with the sword a bit so that Gian Simone would notice it.

Hearing such a nasty response to his question and noticing the weapon he was carrying, Gian Simone surmised at once that he must be a legate. With great pain he decided, on that basis, to sit up and so, in his bed, he opened the notice. He read the summons that said: "On behalf and by command of the Reverend Vicar of the Archbishop of Florence, you, Gian Simone, hatter, are ordered, to pre - sent yourself within three hours to the chancellery of the said bishop's palace under penalty of excommunication and payment of 100 florins per hour of delay." Underneath, Pilucca signed the name of the chancellor, which he knew, and properly affixed it with a badly smeared seal, so that you couldn't see what might have been stamped. It looked as if it had been done in a hurry, which was hardly unusual.

Gian Simone was left utterly surprised and full of sharp pain, and he wondered what this could be about. In the meantime he had his maid bring him his clothes, dressed himself and decided to leave the house that morning at all costs. He said, "You see that I must leave home for something. What the devil do I have to do with the bishop? I know for certain that I don't have anything to share with the priests, the friars, or the monarchs. I can't understand this."

Meanwhile, the Scheggia, who remained at his post watching the house, afraid that Gian Simone might not come out, knocked on the door and was let in. He had no sooner arrived in the bedroom when, almost weeping, he began to say, "Now truly we're utterly ruined. There is no more protection for us! Poor us! Who would have ever guessed? In the end, if I'm delivered from this, never again will I meddle with sorcerers or wizards. What accursed things necromancers and necromancy are!"

More than once Gian Simone pleaded with him to tell him what this was all about, but the Scheggia, continuing his lament, never answered him. Because he heard the necromancer mentioned, he shouted, "Scheggia, for goodness sake, tell me what trouble you're in, and why you're whining so."

"It's the one thing," the Scheggia replied quickly, "that could be as bad for you as for me."

"Alas, what else is new," said Gian Simone. And he wanted to show him the summons when the Scheggia said, "You see this? It is a summons from the Vicar."

"Oh no," replied Gian Simone. "Here's another."

"Here comes your ruin and mine," said the Scheggia.

"Why?" asked Gian Simone. "Tell me at once what's going on here."

So the Scheggia sadly began to explain, "Your companion, the monk, who was carried through the air by demons, as you know, has never stopped pressing this matter like a crazy man. So he heard about the whole thing from Pilucca, exactly how you and I are the principle cause, and how it was all undertaken so that you'd be convinced of Zoroastro's powers. So the monk was furious, and he went to find the vicar yesterday evening to explain the case, and Pilucca testified that it was all true. Therefore it seemed to the vicar that this was something wicked, and he quickly wanted to have the summons made, but because it was late and the chancellor wasn't there he postponed it until this morning. This is what I've just heard from a priest, a very good friend of mine who stays with the vicar. You see, now, where we find ourselves."

"Does it seem so serious to you," asked Gian Simone, "that you ought to suffer such grief and be so afraid? What have we done, anyway?"

"What have we done?" said the Scheggia. "Listen to this. In the first place, we've sinned against the faith by believing in spells, and we've tried by means of demons to disgrace a noble and virtuous woman, and then we endangered the monk's life by having him brought through the air so very far, a thing that still scares him out of his wits and makes him afraid that the devil might possess him. These are all things that are done at the risk of life itself. You can be sure that if we present ourselves to the vicar we'll immediately be put in prison. And confessing our secret will put us in peril of being burned at the stake. But we can't deny it, since they have the proof, and the least that might happen to us would be for us to be pilloried...or paraded upon an ass with a strong condemnation...or perhaps we might have all of our possessions taken from us...or we could be shut up in the basement of a tower... or perhaps something worse. Alas! Does this seems a trifle to you?" At the end of his speech he cunningly cried so many tears that it was a marvel to see, and weeping he said, "Alas, sad Scheggia! Go now and buy your prison cell. If you only had some money handy you could escape, just as the necromancer will do as soon as he hears about this, since I am certain that he wouldn't want to wait for a judgment."

Gian Simone considered what he said, saw how he looked and acted and how he wept, and he firmly believed that what the Scheggia said was true. He was more afraid than ever, thinking that he was in the hands of the inquisitors. Weeping, he began to swear and curse his love, the widow, the necromancers, and necromancy, and he turned to the Scheggia and said, "Pilucca and Zoroastro – what will they do?"

"Pilucca," replied the Scheggia, "is in league with the monk and will be set free as an informer. Zoroastro will go on a long trip someplace far away. But then, he has a thousand ways to escape and also to save us."

"Why don't you go ask him if he wouldn't mind helping us to escape from this fury?" asked Gian Simone. "Alas, it seems worse than before."

"I know what someone could easily say about you," replied the Scheggia. "You've gone from the frying pan into the fire. But what face would I show him, since I failed to deliver the twenty-five florins he was certainly expecting to earn when he demonstrated his powers to you. Although he received your gifts, do you think that he remembers them and that they remained in his heart?"

Gian Simone then said, "Oh God, if he frees us somehow from this mess I'll give the florins to him even now. What good will they ever be? I can't give in to despair."

"Please, Lord, let this make him content," replied the Scheggia, lifting his hands to heaven. "Just now, just now I want to go look for him, but only if you don't object because we're in danger."

"No, don't think about it," added Gian Simone. "Alas, to end up at the mercy of priests! In fact, they'd declare me a heretic and condemn me to the fire. And if I gave them all my possessions and my entire estate, it would seem like a trifle to them. Go on you way, and may God go with you."

The Scheggia left immediately and was happier than ever. He left that house, then, not long after, he returned, pretending that he had spoken to the necromancer. He told Gian Simone that Zoroastro would be willing to do everything, but first he needed the money and then he'd find a thousand ways to free him.

Although Gian Simone regretted spending the money, he was, at the same time, not yet ready to face the vicar and put himself to that test, and he thought that he'd have too much grief if his problems were known throughout the city. So he turned to the Scheggia and said, "The money is in that coffer there. Take it to your post when you wish. But before you take it in your hands, I want to understand how he intends to free us, because I wouldn't like to fall into a sea that's any deeper."

"How wisely and well you speak," replied the Scheggia. "I will go running off to find him and make him tell me how he intends to save us. I'll return to you immediately with his reply. In the meantime, count the money so that I won't have to."

"Okay," said Gian Simone, "I'll do it now while my wife is at mass. Make sure that you come back quickly because every moment I'm involved in this plot feels like a thousand years."

The Scheggia left at once, running full of joy as he went flying to Zoroastro's house. He found him there with Pilucca. Together they were waiting for him, pining away until they could hear how the matter had gone, fearing that the hare might not be led along. But when they heard what he had to say, they felt such joy that they were beside themselves. At last the Scheggia – after he drank a bit of good wine left over from the evening before and having been treated like a champion – came back almost running to Gian Simone's house.

He found Gian Simone in the bedroom waiting for him with the money all counted. After greeting him he said, "This is how Zoroastro plans to set us free, Gian Simone – although there are many other ways that he could use. From speaking with a spirit of his, which he has forced into an vial, he has learned that only Pilucca, the monk, the vicar, and the chancellor know the precise details of this affair, and no one else. And though the chancellor might have made the subpoena, he nevertheless didn't write it in the book, because they aren't accustomed to write them down until either the subpoened individuals appear or the appointed time for them to appear has passed. So, Zoroastro has made four images of green wax, one for each one of them, and has just sent to a demon who is confined in hell in the River Lethe for a carafe of that enchanted water. He'll dip the images in that water three times, then melt and destroy them so that those men will quickly forget everything about our case, and they'll never remember anything of it for the rest of their lives, even if they were to live for a thousand years. And if you or I should say anything, Pilucca and the monk would think we were crazy. There won't be anyone to remind the vicar and the chancellor, nor anyone to press the lawsuit, since they will have all forgotten it, and since they didn't write it down in the book of legal suits, they won't go any farther. And so it will seem as if nothing had ever happened. This is called the spell of oblivion."

These seemed to be wonderful and extraordinary things to Gian Simone, but since he believed that the monk flew through the air to arrive at Zoroastro's house – which was harder to believe – he could believe what the Scheggia told him. So with faith in the Scheggia's false words, he said, "The money is there on the chest in that pillowcase. Take it to your post. But there are only twenty-two florins there, because I spent three between my illness and the gift for Zoroastro. Will we manage?"

"In the name of God," replied the Scheggia, "So that the delay won't cause any problems, I think it would be good if I borrowed the rest of the money from one of my friends, a banker, and added in this borrowed money. What the devil can happen? But this can't wait."

"You'd do well," said Gian Simone, "as soon as you've given the money to Zoroastro and the spell is finished, to

Antonfrancesco Grazzini

come back and let me know." And so, very happily, the Scheggia took the pillowcase with all the gold and silver money and left Gian Simone and went flying to his two companions who were waiting for him. They saw the money and heard about the three missing florins, which the Scheggia said he'd borrow. Laughing and full of joy they decided to have a good time and a happy and hearty celebration for as long as it lasted. It was arranged that Pilucca would go for the monk, and that he would come there for dinner, so everyone could see him again.

The Scheggia returned to Gian Simone and said to him, "Everything's done." Then he went on, "I borrowed the three florins that were missing, and I went away, flying off to the necromancer. I found him just as the devil brought that water. So, as soon as he saw the money, he soaked the images, and then put all four of them over a fire of coals which he had already lit. The images melted and were consumed in an instant. Then, Zoroastro brought in a big basin of enchanted water and said something I couldn't understand, and then he extinguished the fire, and he said to me, "Go back to your house and don't be afraid of anything anymore." I thanked him, quickly departed, and as I was coming to your house, I met the monk precisely at the corner of the Via dei Pazzi. He smiled at me and said, "God be with you," although he never used to speak like that to me. On the contrary, he always gave me a look like that of a harsh stepmother."

Gian Simone was left feeling very content, as you can imagine. And he said to the Scheggia, "Do you believe that if Zoroastro made an image of me, I'd also forget?"

"Certainly you would," replied the Scheggia, "Do you have any doubts?"

Gian Simone said, "I want you to return to him and make him do it, and he can charge whatever he wants. Provided that I can forget this thing, I'll be the happiest man alive."

The Scheggia replied, "Cursed be your thoughtlessness. You could certainly have told me a little while ago. Now it would be much too great a bother to make the devil return and to control him. Isn't it enough that you're free of it? And I certainly wouldn't want to trouble him too much, since he might then have reason to say that I'm a good-for-nothing. Also, I don't want to tempt fate anymore, or to meddle ever again with spirits or with spells or with enchanters. Consequently, you should be patient."

"What you say is true," replied Gian Simone. "This has gone much too far." And after some other similar discussions, he left the Scheggia in peace.

The Scheggia went to Zoroastro's house where his companions were waiting, and he told them everything as he dined merrily with that group. The next day then, Gian Simone went outside and found the monk and Pilucca, and he was convinced about the spell of oblivion. For a while he didn't understand what had happened, and he even tried to avoid them, but they just smiled at him. And the four companions left him with the joke and the damage, and for a long time they had a wonderful time at his expense.

GLOSSARY

🦁

Acquapendente: Small town in the province of Viterbo.

Alfonso, King: (d. 1458) Alfonso V of Aragon (I "The Wise" of Naples) took Naples from the Angevins in 1442. He was later patron of Lorenzo Valla, Gianozzo Manetti, Giovanni Pontano and other noted humanists.

Aragon, Don Juan of: Count of Ripacorsa and viceroy of Naples (1507/8).

Aragon, Federico D': (d. 1504) In 1496, Federico succeeded his nephew Ferdinand II to the throne of Naples, but was driven from rule by the invasion of the French and Spanish in 1501.

Assassins: Fearsome members of a Moslem sect who, under the influence of hashish, murdered Christian leaders in the time of the Crusades.

Bartolo di Giovanni Sonaglini: (d. 1395) Merchant and protagonist of a Sacchetti story (148).

Bernardine, Saint: (1380–1444) Popular Franciscan preacher.

Bevilacqua: The Bevilacqua family was among the wealthiest and most noble families of Verona. There were several members of this family who had distinguished military careers. One example is Galeotto (1374–1441) a *condottiere* in the service of Gian Galeazzo Visconti of Milan.

Bourbon, Duke of: (1490–1527) Switched allegiance from French king to Emperor Charles V in 1523. Commander of imperial forces invading Italy, he was killed while attacking Rome.

Glossary

Bruno: A painter who was a comic hero in Boccaccio's *Decameron*.

Buda: Medieval Hungarian city that later merged with Pest, a city directly across the Danube, to form the present day Budapest.

Buffalmacco: A painter and comic hero in Boccaccio's *Decameron*.

Candlemass: February 2 comemorates the purification of the Virgin, and the presentation of Christ in the Temple.

Capua: Capua is a city in Campania on the Volturno river northwest of Caserta. Raymund of Capua (1330-99) was the confessor and biographer of Saint Catherine of Siena.

Charles of Luxemburg, King of the Romans: Emperor Charles IV (1316–78) crowned 1354.

Charles, Emperor of Germany: (1500–58) King Charles I of Spain (from 1516), and Emperor Charles V (from 1519).

Cimabue: (c.1240-c.1302) Florentine gothic master. The work of his disciple Giotto is often seen as a harbinger of the Renaissance. In contrast, the work of Cimabue was seen as archaic, and the sarcastic nature of this comment in "A Trick Played by The Scheggia on Gian Simone Berrettaio" is obvious.

Compline: After sunset.

Dolcibene: Dolcibene de' Tori was crowned King of the Fools by Emperor Charles IV and was the protagonist of nine of Sacchetti's *Trecentonovelle*.

Ember Days: Ember days are fast days associated with the four seasons and are the Wednesdays, Fridays and Saturdays of the weeks of St. Lucy's Day (Dec. 14), the First Sunday of Lent, Whitsunday, and Holy Cross Day (Sept. 14).

Esi: Jesi, a city in the Marches, was the birthplace of Frederick II of Hohenstaufen. In the Renaissance it was controlled by the Malatesta and later the Sforza.

Glossary

Este, Niccolo d': (d. 1441) Niccolo III was as famous for his political skills as for his cruelty and dissoluteness in his personal life. He ordered the execution of his son Ugo and his second wife, Parisina, after discovering that the two were having an affair. It is believed that he died of poisoning at the hands of Visconti agents in Milan.

Fabriano: A city in the Marches east of Gubbio. Birthplace of the artist Gentile da Fabriano and famous as a center of paper manufacture since the Duecento.

Fermo: City in the Marches near the Adriatic Sea famous for its rich library.

Fiesole: An Etruscan, and later Roman hill city, overlooking Florence.

Flagellants: Members of penitential confraternities who ritually stripped and whipped themselves to bring about reconciliation and reform in medieval towns. They first appeared in Italy in 1260.

Formello: City north of Rome in the Monti Sabatini.

Giotto's Campanile: Refers to the bell tower in the Piazza del Duomo near the cathedral of Santa Maria del Fiore begun by Giotto di Bondone in 1334.

Gonnella: Famous fool in the service of the Marquis Obizzo III d'Este, lord of Ferrara (1317-52) who appeared in a number of Sacchetti's *Trecentonovelle*. Noted by Poggio Bracciolini and Pontano.

Horehound: A common herb with medicinal uses credited with anti-magical properties.

James of Compostela, Saint: According to tradition, the apostle St. James preached the gospel in Spain, and after his death his body was taken there from Jerusalem. Its shrine at Santiago de Compostela was one of the major Christian pilgrimage sites in the Middle Ages.

King of Hungary: Louis I of Anjou (1326–82), known as Louis the Great, king of Hungary and Poland.

Glossary

Lambro: A river in Campania that runs from its source in Monte Scuro to the sea south of Capo Palinuro.

Lethe: One of the six rivers of the underworld, its name means "forgetfulness."

Margaret Island: Situated in the middle of the Danube river between Buda and Pest.

Marsilio, Maestro: Luigi Marsili, (1342–94) Augustinian theologian and humanist.

Matins: Before dawn.

Nola: A city east of Naples, it was the birthplace of the philosopher Giordano Bruno.

Nones: Ninth hour after dawn.

Panigale: Panicale, a small Umbrian town south of Lake Trasimeno.

Patarine: The Patarines were members of an eleventh-century reform movement in Milan, at times allied with the Gregorian reform papacy. By the twelfth century the name "Patarine" was applied to Italian Cathars and other heretics.

Peretola: A town three miles from Florence.

Pinaruolo: The city of Pinarolo near Pavia.

Podesta: A chief magistrate with executive powers, very often from another city, elected in a medieval Italian town or republic.

Policastro: A town in Campania, south of Salerno, on the northern coast of the Gulf of Policastro.

Ponte a Selece: Ponte Sele is in the Piana del Sele south of Palermo.

Pontenara: Pontenaia, a district of Todi in Umbria through which courses the river Naia.

Prime: Dawn.

Saint Catherine's Day: April 29.

Saint George's Day: April 23. St. George is usually depicted with sword in hand slaying a dragon.

Glossary

Saint Michael's Day: (Archangel) May 8.

San Biaggio: Patron of throats, he was a fourth-century bishop and martyr reputed to have performed miraculous cures. His feast day is May 3.

Santa Befania: Befana (see Introduction).

Santa Reparata: Cathedral of Florence in the 10th century on the present site of the cathedral of Santa Maria del Fiore.

Scheggia: Grazzini's favorite protagonist, the Scheggia was the brother of the famous Florentine artist Massaccio (1401–28). He worked in the shop of Bicci di Lorenzo in Florence.

Sernelli, Biagio: Sernello da Montecuccoli, a famous *bon vivant*.

Seven Works of the Mercy: According to Catholic teaching there are seven corporal and seven spiritual works of mercy. The corporal works are to give food to the hungry, give drink to the thirsty, dress the naked, house the homeless, visit the ill, visit the imprisoned, and to bury the dead. The spiritual works are to teach the ignorant, counsel the doubter, console the afflicted, admonish the sinner, pardon offenses, patiently tolerate bothersome people, and to pray to God for the living and the dead.

Sext: Sixth hour after dawn.

Simone, Maestro: Simone Da Villa, who in the *Decameron,* Day 8 Story 9, was the physician who met Bruno and Buffalmacco only to find himself tossed into a ditch and left wallowing in filth.

Tierce: Third hour after dawn.

Ubertino of Carrera: Lord of Padova (d. 1345).

Vespers: Eleventh hour after dawn.

Visconti, Bernabò: (d. 1385) Known as the Tyrant of Mlan.

Visconti, Filippo Maria de': (1392–1447) Duke of Milan whose expansionist ambitions led to years of conflict between Milan, Venice and Florence.

Glossary

Visconti, Galeazzo: Perhaps actually Giangaleazzo known as the Conte di Virtù, duke of Milan (1347–1402). In 1385 he seized his uncle (and father-in-law) Bernabò in an effort to consolidate Visconti rule.

Zara: A Dalmatian port town now known as Zadar.

SELECTED BIBLIOGRAPHY

✣

Primary Sources

Ariosto, Ludovico. *Orlando Furioso*. 2 vol. Trans. Barbara Reynolds. New York: Penguin, 1973 & 1977.

Arlotto, Piovano. "Motti e Facezie." In *Novelle del Quattrocento*. Ed. Aldo Borlenghi. Milan: Rizzoli, 1962.

Bandello, Matteo. *Novelle*. In *Tutte le Opere di Matteo Bandello*. Ed. Francesco Flora. Milan: Mondadori, 1952.

Boccaccio, Giovanni. *The Decameron*. Trans. Mark Musa & Peter Bondanella. New York: Mentor, 1982.

Caro, Annibal. *The Scruffy Scoundrels*. Trans. Massimo Ciavolella & Donald Beecher. Waterloo, Ont.: Carleton University Renaissance Centre & Wilfrid Laurier University Press, 1980.

Castiglione, Baldassare. *The Book of the Courtier*. Trans. George Bull. New York: Penguin, 1967.

Dante Alighieri. *The Divine Comedy*. Trans. Allen Mandelbaum. New York: Bantam Books, 1982.

Firenzuola, Agnolo. *Tales of Firenzuola*. New York: Italica Press, 1987.

Gherardi da Prato, Giovanni. *Il Paradiso degli Alberti*. Ed. Antonio Lanza. Rome: Salerno, 1975.

Gl'Intronati di Siena. "The Deceived." In *Five Italian Renaissance Comedies*. Ed. Bruce Penman. New York: Penguin, 1978.

Selected Bibliography

Grazzini, Antonio Francesco (Il Lasca). *Le Cene.* In *Raccolta de' Novellieri Italiani.* Ed. Carlo Marieni. Milan: Giovanni Silvestri, 1815.

Grazzini, Antonfrancesco. *The Story of Doctor Manente.* Trans. D.H. Lawrence. Florence: Lungarno, 1929.

Manetti, Antonio. *The Fat Woodworker.* Trans. Robert L. Martone & Valerie Martone. New York: Italica Press, 1991.

Medici, Lorenzo (Il Magnifico). "Novella di Giacoppo." In *Tutte le Opere: Scritti Giocosi.* Ed. Gigi Cavalli. Milan: Rizzoli, 1958.

Masuccio Salernitano (Masuccio Guardati). *Il Novellino.* Ed. Giorgio Petrocchi. Firenze: Sansoni, 1957.

Sacchetti, Franco. *Trecentonovelle.* Ed. Vincenzo Pernicone. Florence: Sansoni, 1946.

Sermini, Gentile. *Novelle.* Ed. Aldo Colini. Lanciano: R. Carabba, 1911.

Vinci, Leonardo da. "Favole e Facezie." In *Novelle del Quattrocento* Ed. Aldo Borlenghi. Milan: Rizzoli, 1962.

Secondary Sources

Barolsky, Paul. *Infinite Jest: Wit and Humor in Italian Renaissance Art.* Columbia: University of Missouri Press, 1978.

Baron, Hans. *The Crisis of the Early Italian Renaissance.* Princeton: Princeton University Press, 1966.

Bondanella, Peter, & Julia Conaway Bondanella, eds. *Macmillan Dictionary of Italian Literature.* London: Macmillan, 1979.

Brucker, Gene. *Renaissance Florence.* Berkeley: University of California Press, 1983.

Bullough, G. *Narrative and Dramatic Sources of Shakespeare.* New York: Routledge & Kegan Paul, 1957, 1958.

Selected Bibliography

Burckhardt, Jacob. *The Civilization of the Renaissance in Italy.* Trans. S.G.C. Middlemore. Oxford & London: Phaidon, 1945.

Burke, Peter. *Culture and Society in Renaissance Italy.* New York: Charles Scribner's Sons, 1972.

Clubb, Louise George. *Italian Drama in Shakespeare's Time.* New Haven: Yale University Press, 1989.

Cochrane, E. *Florence in the Forgotten Centuries, 1527-1800.* Chicago: University of Chicago Press, 1973.

Dictionary of Italian Literature. Westport, CT: Greenwood Press, 1979.

Goodman, Paul. "Comic Plots." In *The Structure of Literature.* Ed. Paul Goodman. Chicago: University of Chicago Press, 1954.

Greene, Thomas M. "The Flexibility of the Self in Renaissance Literature." In *The Disciplines of Criticism: Essays in Literary Theory, Interpretation, and History.* Ed. Demetz, Greene, and Nelson. New Haven: Yale University Press, 1968, pp. 241-64.

Guerri, D. *La Corrente Popolare nel Rinascimento. Berte, Berle, e Baie nella Firenze del Brunellesco e del Burchiello.* Florence: Sansoni, 1931.

Hale, J.R., ed. *The Thames and Hudson Encyclopaedia of the Italian Renaissance.* London: Thames and Hudson, 1981.

Hardison, O.B. "The Orator and the Poet: The Dilemma of Humanist Literature." *Journal of Medieval and Renaissance Studies* 1 (1971): 33-44.

Hibbert, Christopher. *The House of Medici: Its Rise and Fall.* New York: Morrow Quill, 1980.

Howard, Donald R. *Chaucer: His Life, His Work, His World.* New York: Fawcett Columbine, 1987.

Jeanneret, Michel. *A Feast of Words: Banquets and Table Talk in the Renaissance.* Trans. Jeremy Whiteley & Emma Hughes. Chicago: University of Chicago Press, 1991.

Selected Bibliography

Larner, Christina. *Witchcraft and Religion: The Politics of Popular Belief.* New York: Blackwell, 1984.

Lee, A.C. *The 'Decameron': Its Sources and Analogues.* New York: Haskell House, 1966.

Levin, Harry. *The Myth of the Golden Age in the Renaissance.* Bloomington: Indiana University Press, 1969.

Logan, Terence P., & Denzell S. Smith, eds. *The Predecessors of Shakespeare: A Survey and Bibliography of Recent Studies in English Renaissance Drama.* Lincoln: University of Nebraska Press, 1973.

Lopez, Robert S. *The Three Ages of the Italian Renaissance.* Charlottesville: University Press of Virginia, 1970.

Marcus, Millicent Joy. *An Allegory of Form: Literary Self-Consciousness in the Decameron.* Stanford French & Italian Studies 18. Stanford: Anma Libri, 1979.

Martines, Lauro. *The Social World of the Italian Humanists, 1390–1460.* Princeton: Princeton University Press, 1963.

Partner, Peter. *Renaissance Rome 1500–1559.* Berkeley & Los Angeles: University of California Press, 1979.

Rodini, R. J. *Antonfrancesco Grazzini, Poet, Dramatist, and Novellieri.* Madison: University of Wisconsin Press, 1970.

Rubenstein, Nicolai, ed. *Florentine Studies: Politics and Society in Renaissance Florence.* Evanston, IL: Northwestern University Press, 1968.

Runciman, Steven. *The Sicilian Vespers.* New York: Cambridge University Press, 1992.

Sanders, Wilbur. *The Dramatist and the Received Idea: Studies in the Plays of Marlowe and Shakespeare.* Cambridge: Cambridge University Press, 1968.

Scribner, B. "Reformation, Carnival, and the World Turned Upside Down." *Social History* 3 (1978): 303-29.

Singleton, Charles S. "On Meaning in the *Decameron*." *Italica* 21 (1944): 117-24.

Selected Bibliography

Smith, Denis Mack. *A History of Sicily: Medieval Sicily 800–1713*. New York: Dorset, 1968.

Tateo, Francesco. "Il 'realismo' nella novella boccaccesca." *Retorica e poetica fra medievo e rinascimento*. Bari: Laterza, 1960, pp. 197-202.

Valency, Maurice, & Harry Levtow, eds. *The Palace of Pleasure: An Anthology of the Novella*. New York: Putnam, 1960.

Vickers, Brian, ed. *Occult and Scientific Mentalities in the Renaissance*. Cambridge & New York: Cambridge University Press, 1984.

Whitrow, G.J. *Time in History*. New York: Oxford University Press, 1989.

Wilkins, Ernest H. *A History of Italian Literature*, 2d ed. Cambridge: Harvard University Press, 1974.

Wright, H. G. *Boccaccio in England from Chaucer to Tennyson*. London: University of London (Athlone), 1957.

Wyrick, Deborah Baker. "The Ass Motif in *The Comedy of Errors* and *A Midsummer Night's Dream*." *Shakespeare Quarterly* 33 (1982): 432-48.

Yates, Frances A. *Theatre of the World*. Chicago: University of Chicago Press, 1969.

This Book Was Completed on April 1, 1994 at
Italica Press, New York, New York and Was
Set in Bembo. It Was Printed on 50 lb
Booktext Natural, Acid-Free Paper
with a Smyth-Sewn Binding
by BookCrafters,
Chelsea, MI
U. S. A.
★ ★
★

OTHER MEDIEVAL & RENAISSANCE TEXTS
PUBLISHED BY ITALICA PRESS

Aldus and His Dream Book, by Helen Barolini

Barbarossa in Italy
Thomas Carson, trans. & ed.

Guido Cavalcanti, *The Complete Poems*
Marc Cirigliano, trans. & ed.

Agnolo Firenzuola, *Tales of Firenzuola*

Luigi Guicciardini, *The Sack of Rome*
James H. Mc Gregor, trans. & ed.

Antonio Manetti, *The Fat Woodworker*
Robert L. & Valerie Martone, trans. & eds.

Petrarch, *The Revolution of Cola di Rienzo*

Visions of Heaven & Hell Before Dante
Eileen Gardiner, ed.

FORTHCOMING
1994
Gaspara Stampa, *Selected Poems*
Laura Anna Stortoni & Mary Prentice Lillie, trans. & eds.

1995
The Miracles of St. James
Linda Davidson, Maryjane Dunn & Thomas F. Coffey,
eds. & trans.